"This is not just a powerful story ~~a practical handbook to equip the~~ mind, and a window *into the heart of God to thrill and bless the spirit –a rich feast!"*

Jennifer Rees Larcombe, author and speaker

"Readable, practical, believable, helpful, and deeply personal: I enjoyed this book, and I believe you will too."

Dr Steve Brady, Moorlands College,

Christchurch

"Despite the fact that I am not given much to crying, I found tears starting to my eyes many times as I read this powerful book. If anyone has the right to speak on resilience, surely it is Debbie Duncan. At one point she writes of the way in which the Hebrews 11 heroes of faith encourage her; in Debbie's life and in her writings we find another hero of faith. She writes with the credibility of one who has suffered deeply and variously without losing her hope and, therefore, her faith in the Christ who gave her life. Her practical applications, woven through as they are with the stories of lives which have touched and influenced her, and highlighted by her own journey with its losses and gains, mean that every prayer and principle she cites is gilded with the luminescence of integrity. She lives the truth she writes of.

"The years and the fears so easily operate like a dripping tap on the life of faith we are called to live. Our joy is eroded, and with it, our resilience. The Art of Daily Resilience provides for us a remedy, should we choose to take the advice of one who has lived that out remedy out through the ups and downs, the failures and the brokenness, as well as the successes and strengths.

This book brings to our remembrance that the joy of the Lord can be our strength, should we choose to do it His way. Debbie doesn't skirt around the fact that the difficult times are part of life but she makes it clear that the overarching message of life in Christ can do more than uphold us; it can make us grow in ways we never could have envisaged. When this book is published, I'll be buying it for gifts. It holds answers many Christians are desperate for."

Bev Murrill, speaker and author

"Rarely do I read a book that gives me as much wisdom as this one does. Debbie has woven together the threads of her life powerfully to craft a tapestry of resilience that is both beautiful and strong. From her experience in the nursing profession she gives us solid, helpful advice on looking after our bodies and our minds. From her many years as a Christian leader she shares profound reflections on how we can lean into God. From her own experiences of life she roots her guidance in the reality of everyday life. This book is a huge help for pastors and counsellors as they seek to understand resilience and help those whom they serve. More than that, however, The Art of Daily Resilience will be a lifeline for anyone who has found life hard, who needs to find a way of strengthening their faith and looking after themselves so that they can face the future with a deeper sense of God's ability to hold them through the fiercest storms."

Malcolm Duncan

"We were crushed and overwhelmed beyond our ability to endure, and we thought we would never live through it. In fact, we expected to die. But as a result, we stopped relying on ourselves and learned to rely only on God, who raises the dead."

2 Corinthians 1:8–9 (NLT)

This book is dedicated to all those people who get up when they fall down and keep going, trusting in the One who made them – and for the families that are there to help them get up, and who run with them.

Malcolm, Matthew, Benjamin, Anna, and Riodhna: thank you.

For Anne, who has shown remarkable resilience these last few years.

I also want to dedicate it to new friends: the Knight family (Peter, Ellie, Joe, Tom, Emma, and Ed) whom we are getting to know. We are so grateful we got to know Louise in a small way – thank you that we can know a little of your story. We are looking forward to what lies ahead.

Thank you, too, Jim Graham, for believing I have a voice and a story to tell.

Contents

Foreword

"How can you pray when you cannot form the words?"

Debbie Duncan is one classy lady: strong, determined, capable, intelligent. This is just as well, because she and Malcolm have faced more than their share of traumas. Their health, and that of their children, has been repeatedly tested to breaking point. There has been a quite horrible series of deaths in their immediate family, and they have had to pick up the pieces, to weep with those who weep, to go on caring.

If this were not enough, Debbie and Malcolm have had the oversight of several large churches, and any pastor will know that most problems in a congregation sooner or later end up at their door.

How do you bounce back? How do you pick yourself up, and carry on? "I have cried so hard that my eyes were raw," Debbie recalls. "My chest was so tight I felt as if I could die from grief. But I didn't."

What has kept her going? The answer is the topic of this book. Debbie explores physical, mental and spiritual resilience, considering how we can become sufficiently robust to meet the challenges we face. We need to take a holistic approach to our problems, she recommends: we are one organism. Exercise, eat well, sleep properly, allow space for rest and prayer: it's all connected.

Debbie writes movingly of her own struggles, not least with depression. Ten per cent of the population will have had at least one episode of depressive illness in the last year.

Christians are far from immune, but churches – evangelical churches in particular – have not been good at recognising and accepting mental illness, regarding it as a sign of spiritual weakness. Debbie calls for an open dialogue.

I found the section on spiritual resilience fascinating. Even the US Air Force recommends training in spiritual resilience! She encourages us to check on our spiritual health, much as we would attend a medical screening or a blood test. She felicitously quotes John Calvin: "Without knowledge of God there is no knowledge of self."

A principle pleasure in this informative book is the blend of sane advice drawn from Debbie's nursing background, with the shrewd insights gleaned from many years of prayer and Bible study. Debbie has an inquisitive mind, and her explorations into the human condition are studded with quotes from her wide reading and happy examples from her long pastoral ministry.

This book is a treat. It's full of hard-won wisdom and practical common sense. Above all, its solutions are within reach. Resilience is not innate; it's an ability to be acquired and fostered. As Debbie says, it's an art.

Tony Collins

Acknowledgments

It's always hard to know where to start when you want to acknowledge people. There's always that fear that you may miss someone out. But there are so many people I want to thank. It has been such a privilege to work alongside you all.

My obvious thanks go to Malcolm, my travelling companion for nearly twenty-five years. Thank you for spurring me on! Thank you for helping me get up when I feel injured and am not sure I can finish the race. I love you more than ever.

Thank you to Matthew, Benjamin, Anna, and Riodhna: my loving children and fan club! And my sister Lorna who has supplied me with endless encouragement. Paul – you are next, get writing!

I want to thank Dave Beattie who helped me shape and sculpture this work. Thank you, Dave, for your patience and wisdom.

I also want to thank Tony Collins who believed I had something worthwhile to say. He helped me develop the seed of an idea into a full-blown book. Thank you to Simon Cox, Jenny Muscat, and the team at Monarch Books.

A huge thank you, too, for those who have walked this walk with me and have helped me create something to share: Jackie Buie, Fiona Castle, Joyce Gledhill, Jane Owen, Jackie Jackson, Amy Boucher Pye, Helen and James Simmons, Stephen and Nicki Walker-Williams, Ruth and Andrew Webber. The list goes on...

I am so grateful for my church family at Gold Hill Baptist Church who have stood with us as a family these last few years.

And Petrova – I told you one day your name would be in a book. Keep aiming high!

CHAPTER 1

Introduction

Have you ever had a day that started with ordinary things but as the day wore on, became extraordinary? When I woke up on 15 November 1999 my thoughts were immediately dominated by the list of jobs I had to do. We were living in Bournemouth at the time and were about to move house. My husband, Malcolm, was the pastor of a thriving local church and we wanted to live in the community where the church was established. Our house sale had been delayed and there were boxes stacked up in the lounge and in every available corner of our home. I even had to negotiate the wall of boxes in our bedroom to extricate my clothes from the wardrobe.

I remember trying to be quiet that morning to allow Malcolm to sleep on for a little while as he had already been up earlier with Riodhna, our three-month-old daughter. (Have you noticed how people always seem to move house when they have a newborn baby?) We finally had a moving date and we were due to move in a couple of weeks' time.

Matthew and Benjamin, our five- and three-year-old sons, had to get dressed and ready for school and nursery. I also had to get Anna, our two-year-old daughter, fed and

13

watered. Thankfully Riodhna was sound asleep like her dad. Our mornings were generally mayhem. I think tiredness is such a lame word to describe the exhaustion we all felt at that time.

I remember that as the noisy yawning sounds of a waking house penetrated my ears, despite the tiredness, I felt grateful that we had this morning all together.

We had had a fairly traumatic six months. It all started when I was pregnant with our last child. I had a horrific delivery and nearly died as I had a low-lying placenta that mainly covered the opening of my womb. Although I had an ultrasound scan the placenta site was never checked, and I had an induced labour for other medical reasons. Then, while in established labour, I haemorrhaged and Malcolm had to choose between mother and child. I have never had to be in that place, making such a decision. It traumatized him as much as the experience traumatized me.

Two weeks after the emergency C-section I woke with terrible abdominal pain. I thought my wound was dehiscing. I ended up back in the operating theatre to have my gall bladder removed due to gallstones. Then, a month later, I came home from physio to discover Malcolm unconscious on the sofa. When I left home that morning I thought he only had a headache. I was told by the medical staff that he had either a brain tumour, an aneurysm, or acute meningitis. What followed was a scary, tear-filled time when I could not really speak to my best friend as he was unconscious and in an isolation ward. I was still dealing with the impact of multiple surgeries on my own body and mind. Some days I came home and fell into bed exhausted and scared I would lose my mind with the pressures of life.

I still had to protect and help four small children and stay positive for a church family that was confused. Why, God, did we have to go through all that? Why should we have so much illness and pain when we were moving house, had a busy church to support, and a seriously ill son? The bleak colours of winter filled my mind as I struggled to make sense of it all. Even now as I reflect on those events I just cannot describe how we felt. It was as though I were walking through indescribable darkness. I never thought I would feel that sort of pain again.

So that November morning in 1999, in the house of boxes, I got up trying to face the normal routine of life again. And what's more, we also had a birthday party to organize as it was to be Benjamin's birthday in two days' time; he would be four years old.

Later that day Malcolm and I drove to Toys R Us to buy some birthday gifts for Benjamin. We wanted to throw him a party but he was not well enough. We were unsure what to do. Malcolm and I stood in front of the birthday cards, surrounded by Beanie Babies, Furbies, and Pokémon characters. We wanted to buy our son a card with "4" on it as we were so grateful to God that Benjamin was still with us. He has a chronic lung condition and there were times when we were told he would have a short life expectancy.

As we stood on the floor in the toy shop the world stood still. Maybe it was because there was no one needing to be fed or dressed or calling for Mummy or Daddy. No noisy house or workplace banter. Maybe we were just exhausted – I don't know why. I just know that we stood and we sobbed and we held each other. Maybe we were grieving for the past few months when our Father felt so far away. Then, in the pain of all we had gone through, fighting for Benjamin to recover from so many bouts of pneumonia in his short life – we realized that he was turning four. We didn't know if we would be able to buy a card with "5" or "6", let alone "7" on it.

Yet in the centre of the storm, standing in the shop, we knew that God was there. In the pain and the confusion of the last few months and years we knew He was holding us. The ordinary day became extraordinary, deeply etched in our memories ready for the time we needed to be reminded of a God who walks with us always – even into a toy shop to choose a birthday card.

Over ten years later

It's three in the morning over ten years later. I know it's mad – I should be in bed – but I quite like this time of day as I know that the family are all where they should be: sound asleep, all four teenagers, husband, and dogs! It's totally quiet apart from the intermittent ticking of a clock on the mantelpiece. The noise it makes is like soft music. It is not challenging me about the fact that I should be in bed, but reminding me that ahead of me I have hours of my day which I can spend in contemplation and devote to regaining my strength.

Recently we have had some very difficult months – they have been the hardest we have ever gone through. I thought our bad time in Bournemouth was the pits but this was indescribably worse. As a family I know we have had our fair share of trauma. We would often laugh at the fact that I am a nurse – yet we have spent long periods of time utilizing the services of the NHS. I honestly thought that I was a strong person and certainly quite resilient, a mixture of a determined woman, a minister's wife, and a mother – all combined with my Celtic blood! I thought I could cope with anything that came my way.

I think really it's been a slow crescendo into the place we are now. I had been living with the challenge of having methicillin-resistant staphylococcus aureus (MRSA), one of those nasty resistant super-bugs, in my lung for a couple of years. My health was becoming more affected by this foreign organism, and was being made worse by asthma. I was determined to keep plodding on and even then had been considering writing about being resilient.

But then Malcolm broke his leg in three places on his first ever sailing holiday. It was a dramatic event requiring the help of a coastguard rescue and a painful trip home. On their own each of these would be difficult events to negotiate, but then four family members died quite suddenly over a period of fifteen months and Malcolm's mum's health started deteriorating, resulting in her needing full-time care. We felt we were surging from one wave of destruction to another. Three of the four funerals were held in the same place within months of each other, with Malcolm taking each one.

The sudden indescribable loss as people you love are taken from you appears in a way you could never anticipate. The world around you stops and you feel like you are looking into the midst of a tornado, the like of which you have never seen before. Huge trees from your landscape hurl across your line of sight. Objects that have seen time pass and go, which you thought would never be displaced. There is darkness, intense emotion, and now and then things whizz past you. You struggle to notice what is happening. Houses or homes pulled up and gutted – swirling grief and pain. These homes, these lives, will never be the same again. How can you go on living when the centre of them is pulled out by its roots? What do you do when the worst things that could happen, happen?

What do you say or do? How can you ensure you have the resilience you need for the journey ahead? When we received bad news the only thing I could do was take deep breaths and remind myself that as I breathed in I was calling on the name of God: *ruach*, the breath of God.

How can you pray when you cannot form the words?

What makes you strong when you have no strength?

I have also found that processing the shock and grief of recent bereavements has left me vulnerable physically. Within a short period of time I usually ended up with a chest infection or pneumonia. Each time I would be so breathless I could not walk down the street. Our church family have been amazing; they have held us tightly enough not to let us fall, but lightly enough to allow us space to be and to breathe.

In these circumstances, while waiting for news, sleep was difficult and anxiety a constant bedfellow. I can think of times when I was willing the minutes to pass quickly, to be in that room with the doctor and to hear whatever the news would be. There has been so much trauma, and so many tears. I know there will be more, but in all honesty I know I will not fall to pieces, I will not break.

Six months ago I thought I knew what to write about resilience. I thought I *was* quite resilient. We have certainly had our challenges as a family and I have only mentioned a few! There are six of us for a start, and we all live busy, full lives. Who can really predict, though, what will happen and how they will they cope?

I have stood and grieved at the graveside of friends and family on a number of occasions. Does grief itself teach us resilience? Gary Stix, the senior editor for *Scientific American*, suggests that when tragedy strikes, most of us ultimately rebound better than might be expected.[1] He recounts the story of Jeannine Brown Miller who was driving home with her husband one night and came upon a police roadblock near the entrance to the Niagara University campus. She saw the lights of an ambulance and knew her seventeen-year-old son, Jonathan, had been out in his car. Something told her she should stop. She asked one of the workers at the scene if it was her son's registration plate, and then a few minutes later a policeman and a chaplain approached her. In that moment she knew. Jeannine never thought she would get through Jonathan's sudden loss but she had amazing support. Five hundred of Jonathan's classmates from his school attended the funeral. He had been a popular boy and a team player for the school. She also found that her faith sustained her. She went back to work after two weeks' compassionate leave. Time has passed and of course she is still devastated, but she is also living. Neuroscientists and psychologists are surprised by the fact that most victims of tragedy soon begin to recover and ultimately emerge largely emotionally intact. It seems that many of us have an amazing amount of natural resilience.

In his article, Stix points us to the work of George A. Bonanno, who is a professor of clinical psychology at Columbia University. Bonanno suggests that some people do indeed have a natural resilience, which is the main component of reactions to grief and trauma. This natural resilience cannot be taught through specialized programmes and there is little research with which to design resilience training.

I don't know if I have natural resilience. I do know that the grief I have experienced during this period of our lives has made me more aware of the spiritual realm. God often feels so much closer when we are weak. There are times when I have felt Heaven touching Earth and I can almost see the shape of God's hands. At such times a beautiful rich sound seems to be playing in my life: the music of Heaven, which lifts the soul. Sometimes the wrong notes that appear out of tune make it richer, more vibrant, adding colour and depth.

During periods of grief I can try to be more resilient – to allow my grief to lead me back to my Maker, to be reminded of who I really am, even though I may be bent out of shape for a while. I have come to the conclusion that, under Heaven, resilience is an art – we use our natural abilities, learn specific skills, cultivate a strong support network, develop positivity and a confidence that we are in control. It is something we can learn through experience and apply on a daily basis.

What is resilience?

Resilience is a term we use to express how we can bounce back from an awful event or personal tragedy. It is about having the personal strength to complete the course, to reach the end of the road. It is not a concrete asset, something we learn once and then we use again. Our resilience may vary over time.

Dr Tony Newman, principal research and development officer at children's charity Barnardo's, studies the resilience of children. He observes: "Resilience is a quality that helps individuals or communities resist and recover from adversities."[2] We can use it to describe people, organizations, and communities who have the ability to recover their original form. Most of our present understanding of resilience is drawn from studies of children brought up in severe poverty, war zones, or abusive situations, who show they can survive a terrible upbringing and go on even to thrive.

In 1989 the world was first made aware of the Romanian orphanages where children were placed because the state believed it could care for them better than their parents. Visinel Balan was one of these children, shut away in an orphanage, first in Bacăuc and later in Comănești. His earliest memories are of rocking himself backwards and forwards, and of waking up to the sensation of warm urine and knowing he would be beaten on the soles of his feet for wetting the bed.

The adult Visinel now has two degrees in theatre and law and is studying for a Masters in psychology. He owns an apartment and a car, and has started a charity showing people how they can develop their own future. Nothing about him suggests he had a horrific childhood. He is an educated, confident young man, but he believes that within the adult the child is still there. How did he grow into the man he now is? He is unusual in having had survival skills that helped him to escape his previous life. He says at the end of an interview in *The Guardian* newspaper: "No matter where we grew up, we are all human beings."[3]

Visinel's story demonstrates that people can overcome the most terrible of backgrounds and thrive, even without the strength God can give them. It's good to celebrate this attribute in human beings, but we want to focus in on the processes by which resilience can be increased. What difference does being a child of God mean to us? What enables someone not just to cope under pressure, but thrive? How can we develop these qualities? As disciples of Christ, do we need, and receive, particular strengths?

A bruised reed will not break

I was thinking about this topic recently while in the Vendée, in France. We were at a well-known Christian campsite where Malcolm had been speaking all week. I had the privilege of listening to and praying with people there who just needed to recharge their batteries. Some of the people we met were going through some hard situations, and I marvelled at their resilience.

Close to our caravan was a river aptly called the "River of Life", as it was a place where God was refreshing people. One day I walked along the path beside the river, watching my daughter and her friend in their canoe, and found a patch of marshy grass where there were some tall reeds gently swaying in the afternoon breeze, bending to the wind but returning to their position. I could see myself in the reeds, bending but not breaking. I often think of the verse in Isaiah 42:3: "a bruised reed he will not break". If I have learned anything, it is that we won't break. God will not break us.

There are times during periods of bereavement when I have cried so hard that my eyes were raw, and my chest so tight that I felt as if I could die from grief. But I didn't. As a bruised reed we will not break, but as a Christian we never go back to the same shape. God changes us. His Spirit works in us, changing us from one degree of glory to another, a part of ongoing sanctification (2 Corinthians 3:7–8). We don't stand still because God's Spirit changes us. This started the day we asked Him into our lives as an ongoing act of grace. The more we know Him or learn about Him, the more we are changed to be like Him. Our inner nature is changed day by day (2 Corinthians 4:6).

Not only do we reflect or mirror His glory, we will one day be transformed to be like Him, but we are also being daily transformed by the working of His Spirit in us (Philippians 3:20–21; John 3:2; 1 Thessalonians 5:23). If our lives are like a bruised reed that will not break, we can also say that we are not the same people we once were, bending back to the same place or person we were.

I think another picture would be that of an elastic band that can be stretched out of shape and may never go back to the shape it was originally.

A couple of years ago my friend Jackie and I were teaching a group of Bible translators in Kenya about resilience. I was humbled by the fact I was there in the first place. These people worked in a rural setting with few modern facilities. As a nurse educator I always ask about health. I was horrified to hear that parents worried that their children had the symptoms of malaria on a regular basis. There, an infant up to the age of five has on average at least one viral infection a month. The anxiety about it was palpable in the room. I was trying to give them strategies so that they might learn how to reduce this. Wanting to leave them with a visual aid, my friend and I handed them an elastic band each. On reflection, the drawback of this image is that the band gradually loses its elasticity and can no longer stretch. Perhaps a better picture would be that of a muscle that can be stretched and grow stronger every time it is used. I doubt, however, that we could have given them a muscle to take home.

We wanted to say to them: "Increase your resilience. Things will still be difficult and risky and you may feel out of shape as your circumstances stretch you, but you will not break." I don't know if it helped. I do know I was challenged to encourage these families to have good strategies to improve and support their physical health! Resilience is not just about supporting our mental health.

Body, soul, and mind

It is a common convention to divorce the physical realm from the spiritual one. As humans, however, we are made in God's image; He is a tripartite God (Genesis 1:26–27), and our tripartite make-up consists of a body, a soul, and a mind. The body is our physical being or in Greek, our σῶμα – *soma*. My brown hair and blue/green eyes are part of my physical body. The soul is our "psyche" or our mind and conscience. We know from Genesis 2:7 that human beings have a living soul. In philosophy the soul can be considered as the centre of our emotions or our heart. Plato and Aristotle considered that we are dualistic – consisting of only body and soul. Plato, however, believed that a soul may have many bodies, migrating from one to another. Modern Western thinking, meanwhile, is based on the work of René

Descartes who identified that people have a consciousness and self-awareness. The body and mind are thought to exist in the physical realm. An individual's spirit or soul would be embedded in this physical domain as part of this, although there have been questions about how consciousness could be a physical feature of the brain. Philosopher Colin McGinn suggests that neurones and synapses seem "the wrong kind" of material to produce consciousness.[4]

There is a growing movement in sociology to highlight that human beings have a spiritual need, but this school of thought tends to focus on the attitudes and practices which people have as they search for meaning in life.[5] It does imply some kind of vision of the human spirit and of what will help it to achieve its full potential.[6] In fact, spirituality can be regarded as a search for meaning in life with or without God. The spirit is not itself identified as a separate entity. Yet, despite this widespread view, it seems strange that people who do not believe that they have a spirit can nevertheless believe in spiritual powers and evil spirits.

As human beings we have a body and a mind but also a spirit, or pneuma. *Pneuma* (πνευμα) is the Greek word for "breath", and refers to one's spirit or soul. We are made in the image of our Maker. These three parts interweave and interact with each other. Each can also impact the other. A clear example of this is when someone experiences grief. In our society we don't always appreciate that grief is a significant event. Jesus took time out to grieve. We are often expected to function as normal within a very short space of time. Weeks later people often develop a range of physical and psychological conditions as each body-mind-spirit component impacts the other.

There have been times of bereavement in our lives when I have been emotionally distraught but physically able to eat and sleep. As weeks passed and we dealt with the ongoing trauma my body was nevertheless impacted by the stress of grief and bereavement. After a week my immune system was impaired, with reduced numbers of neutrophils in my bloodstream to protect me from infection and raised levels of the stress hormone cortisol. The result was that I caught an upper respiratory infection – it occurred after each of those four deaths.

We know that the emotional stress of grief can lead to the immune system being suppressed, making us more vulnerable to infections. This was highlighted in an article by the journalist Richard Gray that was printed in the *Daily Telegraph* in 2002.[7] He reported that during times of bereavement grieving relatives are more vulnerable to infections. He illustrates this with examples of some well-known figures, such as the former UK Prime Minister James Callaghan who died of pneumonia aged ninety-two, just ten days after his wife, Audrey, had passed away. We are reminded of the instances of husbands and wives who died within days of their loved ones, such as the musician Johnny Cash, who died four months after his wife, June, in 2003.

We are aware that body, mind, and spirit interact. To strengthen our overall resilience we need to learn how to improve resilience in each of these areas. In the following chapters we will look at how we can separate out our physical, mental, and spiritual sides and consider how we can improve resilience in each of these domains.

We also know that resilience is not static: it is not a concrete concept but is organic, growing and changing.

Learning how we can improve resilience may mean looking in depth at some of the notes or sounds we don't feel comfortable with from the music playing in our lives. On other occasions this exercise will be exciting, challenging, and will make us smile. Developing the art of daily resilience means we are allowing ourselves time to see the colours develop like a Polaroid photograph.

PRAYER

Dear Father,

I come before You today, aware that I am made in Your image. I know that I am of mind, body, and soul. I am in need of You working in my life. Hold my heart within Yours, and renew my mind, body, and soul.

Guide me toward better health, and give me the wisdom to know how I can make changes to do this.

Lead me to spiritual well-being. What can I learn to be strong in You?

Direct me to mental wellness. I want to know how I can keep focused on You.

Through the work of Your Spirit and in Jesus' name,

Amen.

CHAPTER 2

The Interaction of Body, Soul, and Mind

A person can be regarded as consisting of three constituent parts: body, soul, and mind. We remember this when trauma happens or when we become stressed about events that occur in our lives. Who would feel that it was an important priority to eat regular meals or take some exercise when they have just heard the news that they have lost their job or when they are thinking of a bill that's due, knowing that they can't pay it? Instead we tend to focus on the problem immediately facing us rather than ensuring that we are robust enough in all areas of our health to cope with what life is throwing at us.

I am a qualified nurse and a lecturer in nursing. During my training years, as we studied a variety of theories of care, we were encouraged to look after people in a holistic manner. And indeed, this is the foundational philosophy that underpins much of nursing today: caring for the whole person – body, soul, and mind.

In the past, however, this approach was distinctly

different from that of my medical colleagues who tended to concentrate on a patient's specific ailment rather than the whole person. Until the later part of the twentieth century, if a patient had a sore foot the doctor would diagnose the condition and hopefully treat the physical complaint. The background to the foot injury would not have been investigated, nor would the likelihood that the resulting anxiety and reduced mobility would be almost certain to impact the practical day-to-day aspects of the patient's job. This approach to medical care is known as the **biomedical model** or the **medical model**.

The American psychiatrist, George Engel, described this model as the framework that doctors of the time used in dealing with disease.[1] It omits the psychological, social, and behavioural aspects of illness and focuses instead on the physical processes, namely the pathology, the biochemistry, and the physiology of disease. The main pillars of this model are considered to be the concepts of pathology, cure, and prevention. For adherents of this model, the roles of social factors or of individual subjectivity are not perceived to be important.

The story of Mrs Jones illustrates this. Mrs Jones has asthma and it has become considerably worse in the past three weeks. Asthma is a disease of triggers, meaning that certain triggering factors generate an immune response in a person's airways, causing symptoms of wheezing and coughing. Followers of the medical model would treat the illness by giving Mrs Jones medication, but might not consider that she is anxious about losing her job. And anxiety itself is a trigger of the disease.

The (bio)medical model is useful in diagnostic medicine

and in the treatment of life-threatening illnesses, but the patient's mental and spiritual well-being are not considered.[2] When people are diagnosed with a life-threatening disease they have to deal with major fear and anxiety about how they will manage or how they will cope with the treatment. This may in turn impact the decisions they make about their health.

Thankfully, that model of medical care has changed and today I meet many doctors who now adopt a more holistic approach to care; nurses and doctors now favour the **biopsychosocial model**, which includes expertise from the pure and psychosocial sciences. The model considers health and illness on three levels – biological, psychological, and social.[3] Illness does not stand in isolation; it affects the body but can also affect the person's mind and social circumstances (and arguably "spirit").

An example of how these three areas are taken seriously is outlined in the Ottawa Charter, an important document produced by the World Health Organization (WHO) in 1986 at their first international conference on health promotion.[4] It suggests that a person's health is dependent on their physical, mental, and social well-being.[5]

In Western medicine it could be argued that Florence Nightingale was the original holistic practitioner. In *Notes on Nursing* (originally published in 1859), she outlined the responsibility of a nurse as caring for the body, soul, and mind. Her personal faith and beliefs impacted her theory about how we should care for people, and she considered this to be the core competency of nursing. She believed in the call to embody the Sermon on the Mount, as recorded for us in Matthew's Gospel.[6]

In describing Florence Nightingale as the original modern-day holistic practitioner, it is important to note that the term "holism" was not widely used until Jan Smuts discussed the link between nature and science in his book *Holism and Evolution* in 1926.[7] The term "holism" comes from the Greek ὅλος (*holos*) meaning "all, whole or entire".

In 1998 Fiona Patterson adopted the term "holism" in her article published in the *Journal of Advanced Nursing*.[8] She described holism as the whole person being more important than the individual functioning parts. Until Patterson's article, holism had been linked with New Age or complementary practices, and holism and holistic care were not considered an important part of how people cared for one another. Nursing theorist Jean Watson has expanded on this idea, calling it a "transpersonal" approach to care where a person consists of more than just their physical body but also consists of spirit and mind – that is, "holism".[9]

In philosophy, particularly metaphysical and early Jewish theology, the body, soul, and mind were strongly linked. Far from being a new practice, holism was already firmly embedded in the Jewish way of life, where there is a strong emphasis on the desire to connect all parts of the self – mind, heart, and body – to the soul and the purpose of life. Judaism requires its followers to follow the "mitzvah" (or the biblical term מצוה (*miswa*), which means commandment). There are 613 commandments given in the Torah, including the Ten Commandments, the Covenant Code, the Ritual Decalogue, the Priestly Code, the Holiness Code, and the Deuteronomy Code. The Jewish nation under Moses declared that it would accept the Law given at Mount Sinai as being central to its faith. Through the rabbinic councils and over time these have increased to 620 moral laws from the original commandments set out in Exodus 20.

I mention this because the Hebrew word "mitzvah" also refers to a moral deed performed as a religious duty or act of human kindness. The tertiary meaning of "mitzvah" also relates to the "fulfilment of a mitzvah". Its root means "connection" where the act of following the law is considered to be an act of the body, soul, and mind. In Judaism, life is called *asher tihiyu*, which conveys the idea of something that is "to be lived". Living out faith in this way encompasses anthropology, theology, philosophy, metaphysics, and psychology. It is therefore holistic and there is an inherent expectation that believers think with their heart, their body, and their soul – not just with their intellect.

As a fascinating aside, when Ethiopian Jews arrived in Israel during the 1980s after the trauma of famine and starvation, the Israeli psychologists and psychiatrists trying to help them discovered that they could not understand the psychology and illnesses of the new immigrants because the practitioners were unfamiliar with the context from which they originated. This proves that each individual needs to be understood in the framework of their personal beliefs and culture.

In contrast to Judaism where the heart of a person is holistic, later philosphers such as the Frenchman, René Descartes, influenced by the early Greek philosophers, presented a person's intellect or decision-making process as a single entity, as summed up in his famous dictum: "I think therefore I am".[10] Although our intellect is important, and it is right to make decisions based on fact and experience, Hebrew culture also expects us to think with the heart, the body, and the soul. This way of life is one of the foundations of our Christian faith.

In chapter 22 of the Gospel of Matthew, Jesus summed up the Law when he was asked by an expert in the Law to state the greatest commandment. His reply in verse 37 is: "Love the Lord your God with all your heart and with all your soul and with your [entire] mind."[11] He then added (verse 40): "All the Law and the Prophets hang on these two commandments." Although Jesus' death and resurrection meant that the requirements of the Law were fulfilled, our response should still be a holistic one; one that requires us to use the indivisible wholeness of our body, soul, and mind.

When I think of this response I often consider an image I had of my daughter playing in the garden. She was twirling around, oblivious to who was watching her and singing at the top of her voice. Her mind, body, and soul were in unison as she sang and danced. I cannot even remember what she was singing. Perhaps it was a song we had sung that morning in church. All three parts of her being were in unison, responding to a tripartite God and reflecting the words of Psalm 84:2: "my heart and my flesh cry out for the living God." She has been blessed with a beautiful voice and sometimes she sings in our worship group. Nowadays she does not twirl around in the afternoon sun but her face lights up as she sings the words of songs that touch her soul.

If we try to separate this connection, then things are not as beautiful or as radiant as they should be. How many of us have listened to someone singing and their face does not mirror the words of their song?

Malcolm and I were once in Rome for a city break. It was actually his thirtieth birthday and I had saved all year so I could surprise him with the holiday. We were out for a walk one evening looking for somewhere to have a meal when we saw a sign in English outside a cathedral, inviting us to hear an American choir singing there that evening. In fact, the concert was about to start so we decided to head in and put off having some food until later. There must have been a thousand people in the cathedral – a beautiful old building – and we were seated waiting to hear a free concert. Not bad! There were lots of whispered, excited voices waiting for the choir to start. And then, when they started singing, you could hear a pin drop. It was not because they sang beautifully – it was because they were terrible! After the first couple of songs, there seemed to be a natural break in the programme. Malcolm suggested we leave – at the same time as about 500 other people!

We headed down the steps, hoping to escape to a lovely Italian restaurant, when we saw a poor family sitting nearby, obviously begging. There was a husband, wife, and infant. As we tried to decide how to help them, two Roman Catholic priests suddenly appeared with a large medicine bag. We could not hear or even understand what they were saying. One brought out a little camping stove, a pot, and some food and started making a meal. The other pulled out a battered Bible from inside his robes and started reading a passage of Scripture to them. At that moment in time it felt as if a little bit of Heaven had touched Earth in that street in Rome. This little family was being fed in body, soul, and mind on the steps in front of a cathedral in Rome. We were bystanders witnessing acts of human kindness – the "mitzvah" or a connection was happening before our eyes.

David Bohm (1917–92) was an American scientist who

has been described as one of the most significant theoretical physicists of the twentieth century. He applied unorthodox ideas in metaphysics to quantum theory, neuropsychology, and philosophy and had a chequered career. In 1943 Bohm joined the Manhattan Project in the United States, contributing to the development of the atom bombs that were dropped on Hiroshima and Nagasaki.

After the war Bohm became assistant professor at Princeton University where he worked closely with Albert Einstein. In 1949 Bohm refused to testify against Robert Oppenheimer, one of his former colleagues who was accused of being a Communist sympathizer, before the House Un-American Activities Committee. Bohm was arrested and sent for trial and although he was acquitted, he was dismissed from his post at Princeton and even Albert Einstein could not persuade the university to reinstate him. A victim of McCarthyism, and unable to work in the United States, Bohm moved to Brazil, Israel, and then England.

His seminal work, *Wholeness and the Implicate Order*, was published in 1980.[12] In his introduction, Bohm wrote that "at each stage the proper order of operation of the mind requires an overall grasp of what is generally known, not only in formal, logical, mathematical terms, but also intuitively, in images, feelings, poetic use of language, etc." He believed that the human mind could only fully function in a generally harmonious way if *all* aspects of the brain were used. He was convinced that a person needs to use their intellect, experience, and spiritual nature, and that this in turn would help to facilitate an orderly and stable society. Not only is the person whole, but society is helped too.

What happens when there is a disconnect between these three areas?

It is helpful to reflect on what happens when the body, soul, and mind are not connected. We can focus exclusively on one method of fulfilment and so forget that we need to have a balance. An example of this is the exercise-obsessed man spending all his time keeping physically fit while not thinking about – and so neglecting – his spiritual nature.

I am reminded of an amusing incident a few years ago when I was at the gym. I was lifting weights at the time and was really concentrating on what I was doing. I was conscious of being the only middle-aged woman in the midst of all these body-builder men! A middle-aged gentleman entered the weights area, complaining loudly about the choice of background music. I looked up to see him and he reminded me of a stereotypical Christian gentleman – the sort who wears white socks and sandals, a pair of tan shorts, and a faded T-shirt that looked as if it were promoting some Christian festival or other.

I cringed. I was there on one of my three weekly visits to keep fit. My face was bright red and sweating, my legs ached and I did not want to start thinking about the inappropriate songs being played. I certainly did not want people to know I was the pastor's wife. To be fair to the gentleman, it wasn't a nice song. I didn't agree with the words. Somehow I had achieved a disconnect between the three areas of my life. While this did not have a *serious* impact on me on that occasion, there are times when it might do so. We can be so focused on one area of our lives that the other parts are neglected. This imbalance can cause us more problems and make us less resilient as we face up to the challenges of life.

In the spring of 1990 I was in the third year of a nursing degree at university in Dundee. At that time I was suffering from clinical depression. Several areas of my life were in imbalance in the months leading up to the crisis. I find it so hard to describe how I felt. It was like living at the bottom of a well or a deep, deep pit where occasionally I would see light. Each day was endless, rolling into another with no end to the sadness I felt. My happiness had become so entwined with my circumstances. There were days when the only way I could see a path out was to take an overdose. I felt like this even though I knew that God loved me.

The background at that time was that I was suffering from reactive depression. I had broken off an engagement to a young man I knew I should not marry. The distress and hurt I was causing were like wounds to my own fragile self-esteem and self-worth. I wondered if I would ever meet someone again who would want to marry me. The church family that I loved could not help me as there had been a church split. The church leadership was in turmoil. I told no one what was happening. I was lonely – and then I heard that my beloved grandad was dying of cancer.

My own parents were in the north of Scotland – a ten-hour train journey away. I had no free time to go home as I was on nursing placement. I was also working as a student nurse in a ward I did not like. Spiritually I was dry, mentally I was challenged, and physically I was exhausted from lack of sleep. Something had to bend under the pressure. This time it was my mind – but it did not break completely. Through months of a blend of friendship, reading the psalms and shouting out to God like the psalmists, medication, and rest, the fog of despair gradually thinned out. I had become bent out of shape. I am so grateful to one particular friend who was not always demonstrative but who would scoop me up and take me to the cinema or out for a walk. All through the summer months God slowly helped me to return to who I was, but I had changed – rather like the illustration of the elastic band in Chapter 1. At the start of the new academic year one of my friends I had not seen for several months remarked that I was somehow different.

I am grateful that I have never had the struggle with mental illness that others have, but at the same time I am glad for the insight into that world. I have been aware that there have been times when anxiety and depression have been close companions but I have developed strategies to recognize when those symptoms have begun to appear and sought to address any imbalance in me. I am not saying that mental illness can always be prevented. What I am saying is that we need to be aware that our body, soul, and mind interact and connect. We need to consider each area and how we can become more resilient in each one.

REFLECTION

> Take time out to reflect whether there are areas in our lives that need more attention than we are giving. There are times when I know I do not read Scripture as I should to feed my spiritual nature. What are your challenges? Ask God to give you wisdom and discernment.

PRAYER

Father,

Thank You for reminding us that we are fearfully and wonderfully made, each part interlinking and interacting with the other.

Help us to know when our lives are out of balance and to turn to You to help us. We often cannot make these changes by ourselves.

Help us to be reliant on Your Spirit's power.

Through Jesus' name,

Amen.

SECTION ONE

Increasing Our Physical Resilience

CHAPTER 3

How Can We Increase Our Physical Resilience?

We know that resilience is a person's ability to respond to a stressful event in a healthy way. It enables us to achieve our goals with minimal psychological and physical cost.[1] Physical resilience has been defined by John Davy as "our ability to maintain or improve function in response to illness, accidents or age-related changes."[2] In that same article about ageing, Davy suggests that improving physical resilience can improve overall resilience in the elderly, and it can also be used as a measure of overall well-being.

In their book *The Peace of Mind Prescription*, the physicians Dennis Charney and Charles Nemeroff list the key components of resilience.[3] They describe physical resilience as physical "toughening" and "tempering" and suggest that people who are physically tough are able to withstand prolonged stress better than those who aren't. If someone is physically fit they may have lower blood pressure, normal blood sugar, decreased anxiety and depression, and a normal sleep pattern. If their bodies are assaulted by what life throws at them, they then have the physical reserves to deal with an attack.

When I think of physical resilience I have a picture of an athlete preparing for a marathon or a national sports competition. I remember watching some of the interviews of Team GB members during the 2012 Olympics and hearing about their commitment to their training. In the past I have not necessarily considered physical training something I have needed to do. I have been in awe of friends who have achieved things such as completing marathons or climbing mountains.

I recently met a lady who was intending to climb Mount Kilimanjaro to fundraise for children in Uganda through the charity she works for. Friends and I were surprised that she had done minimal training for the challenge and was even anaemic. We tried to encourage her to have a medical before she attempted the climb, which she did eventually have before attempting the feat.

Yesterday I chatted to someone who was telling me about the training regime they had in place for running the London Marathon – and what a contrast to the mountain climber! The general recommendation when preparing to run a marathon is to train for six months to a year. As a minimum the experts suggest twenty-six weeks of training, which is equivalent to one week for every mile of the race. Of course, these guidelines depend on an individual's previous training and fitness level.

Typically, those signing up to run any race like a marathon commit themselves to long periods of meticulous preparation, a well thought-out, carefully planned diet, and a programme of progressively longer runs. There are people who claim to have run a marathon without any training, such as the Irish pop duo Jedward – John and Edward Grimes. On national television they said they had completed the Los Angeles Marathon with no training. They simply decided to do it. Another who claims to have taken a similar approach is the former elite athlete David Bedford who, while out clubbing with a friend in the early hours of the morning on the day of the race, decided to enter the 1981 London Marathon. His friend challenged him to do it and Bedford foolishly accepted. He had a curry, got changed, attempted the race, and was even filmed being physically sick halfway round the course. Attempting such a race with no training has huge medical implications, ranging from dehydration to cramps, soft-tissue injuries, vomiting, and even death.

My friend Joyce did a lot of regular exercise (and indeed she still does) before she even considered signing up for a marathon. It even meant that she had to get up at 4 a.m. to do a four-hour run while on a weekend away with friends because she would not have had any other time to train that weekend. Her husband kindly woke her and prodded her to go and train.

No, I have never been a person mad about exercise although I know it has huge health and psychological benefits. I have, however, joined a gym and during periods of wellness I go every day. I particularly love exercising while watching daytime TV!

Words like endurance, strength, and exercise-tolerance come to my mind as I think of what exercise means to our bodies. Not only do professional athletes consider their fitness regimes but they also look at their sleep patterns and rest, diet and nutritional state, and general physical well-being. Now

I am not suggesting that we all sign up to do a marathon – what I *am* suggesting is that we can learn a lesson from these competitors. They plan and train for an event that will challenge their bodies. And life is a challenge. We all know that things can change in a heartbeat. We can wake and get dressed for a normal day but within seconds a telephone call can change everything: a relative has died in tragic circumstances; a friend has been in a traffic accident. Our world is turned upside down and our body suffers from an assault that feels like a physical attack. And so it is: a bomb has detonated in our landscape and our body feels the full shock of it.

In the 1920s the American physiologist Walter Cannon suggested that the human body goes through a physiological reaction when faced with acute stress. He initially observed animals in the wild and noted a cluster of common physiological responses that occurred when they were frightened. He then transferred this to humans, coining the notion of the "fight-or-flight" response to acute anxiety or fear. This chain of rapidly occurring reactions within the body happens to allow us to adapt to acute circumstances. The adrenal medulla within the brain rapidly produces a hormonal cascade that results in the secretion of catecholamines – the commonest of which are adrenaline and noradrenaline. These chemicals act on our heart muscles, causing an increase in the heart rate as oxygen is pumped faster around the body, and they trigger the release of glucose from our fat stores, increasing the blood flow to skeletal muscle. The body is in fact primed for "fight or flight". Although this is an adaptive reaction to an acute event, prolonged stress can cause a variety of negative physiological effects, some of which are listed below:

- headaches
- muscle tension
- chest pain
- fatigue
- altered sex drive
- gastric symptoms
- altered sleep patterns
- urinary problems
- altered menstrual patterns.

Prolonged stress can also impact the immune system, making it more difficult to recover from an infection or heightening susceptibility to disease. Recovery can be slow and debilitating.

So how can we ensure that our bodies are more resilient to run the race that we are in? There are some practical things we can do without necessarily adhering to an athlete's complex plan. Let's look at them here and in the following chapters.

Exercise

Every day we are bombarded with bogus claims about the benefits of quick workouts. Fitness infomercials seduce us into believing that if we use the advertized equipment for so many minutes a day, we will look like the models demonstrating the product. The UK's National Health Service (NHS) recommends that adults aged 19–64 should do 150 minutes of physical activity a week[4] – that is, thirty minutes, five days a week.

It is recommended that you do two types of physical activity each week: aerobic and muscle-strengthening. Aerobic activity can be exercise such as running, cycling, or a game of singles tennis. Muscle-strengthening activity includes lifting weights, working with resistance bands, or even heavy gardening.

The WHO makes similar recommendations:

> adults aged 18–64 should do at least 150 minutes of moderate-intensity aerobic physical activity throughout the week or at least 75 minutes of vigorous-intensity aerobic physical activity throughout the week or an equivalent combination of moderate- and vigorous-intensity activity.[5]

This level of exercise will give you cardiac protection and reduce the risk of heart disease.

Regular physical activity makes your body produce more energy. In the short term it can help you sharpen your focus for up to two to three hours after the event. The benefits of longer-term exercise are that men and women who are more active have lower rates of heart disease, hip, or vertebral fractures, high blood pressure, stroke, type-2 diabetes, colon and breast cancer, and a reduced risk of developing Alzheimer's disease and depression.

There is also evidence to show that exercise helps us increase our self-control. In research conducted at the University of Exeter in 2009, twenty-five chocolate lovers were put through a mini-stress test looking at self-control and exercise.[6] A fifteen-minute walk helped people cope better with stress than resorting to their usual dose of chocolate.

We are also aware that exercise can help improve our psychological well-being. Even a five-minute walk in the fresh air can lift our self-esteem and mood.[7] This is helpful to know as there are people who, like me nowadays, do not exercise regularly and can be intimidated or overwhelmed by the evidence-based guidelines for physical activity. We know the advice and the benefits but physical fitness is one of our biggest stumbling blocks. We all know it is something that will make a long-term difference to our lives but many of us struggle to slot it into our weekly timetable.

You may be like me and struggle with chronic illness or physical disability that means you cannot do what you used to do. I would suggest that you seek medical advice about what exercise programme can be tailored to your needs. One example is that GP surgeries link into local recreational providers and can provide an exercise referral scheme. For me it has meant taking little steps to be able to achieve larger ones in the future. Sometimes I park my car a little further away from my destination than I need to, so I have to walk a little further.

Even short sessions of exercise of five to fifteen minutes a day have been shown to have benefits for physical and mental health. Baby steps are what we need to take. In a medical research study from 2006, M. A. Guidry and colleagues support the idea that short doses of low-intensity exercise, especially when performed in the morning, could provide significant cardiovascular health benefits to a sedentary population.[8]

There are also specific exercise programmes we can use. A Harvard Medical School study has shown that people who did yoga are less prone to angry outbursts and are more resilient than those who took part in other exercise programmes.[9] Yoga has been found to be helpful as people slowly build their endurance and ability to deal with inner turmoil. We know that yoga involves strengthening and improving the flexibility of the muscles but the philosophy behind yoga is that the path to spiritual growth and enlightenment opens up during the exercises. The goal is to unite one's temporary self with the Hindu concept of God called Brahman. This is a pantheistic belief that everything is God, and is separate from the Christian belief that there is one God and one way to God through Jesus Christ His son. There are, however, forms of yoga where the spiritual focus is more in line with the Christian faith.

So what is known to help combat anxiety and depression is the combination of physical exercise and spiritual meditation.

It is important to find out what sort of programme works best for us. To do so, ideally we need to be aware of our natural biorhythms. Some people exercise better in the mornings, while others prefer an evening swim. We should choose something that we enjoy and that fits into our lifestyle.

In summary, it is recommended that we try to remain physically fit. This does not mean that we train like a weightlifter. We know that being physically strong does help us deal with some of life's challenges. If our body is strong, then we have the strength and endurance to have a stronger mind. We can try a simple change to our routine, such as taking a walk in the sunshine for twenty minutes a day. This has been shown to help people be more open-minded and ready to face change.[10]

Diet and nutrition

We have all had those days when breakfast is a cup of coffee and lunch, eaten as we sit hunched over a desk, is a pre-packed sandwich loaded with salt and calories. I think a good illustration is that our bodies are like cars that need to be fuelled before they go on a journey. Eating a healthy diet is easy – it's sticking to it that's hard. We are recommended to eat a diet based on starchy foods such as potatoes, bread, rice and pasta, plenty of fruit and vegetables, some protein-rich foods such as meat, fish, and lentils, some dairy foods, and not too much fat, salt, or sugar. According to NHS Choices, this will provide us with all the nutrients we will need.[11] The key is to have the right balance of a variety of foods in the right proportions. I have to confess that when I am not attending a slimming group I do consume the wrong amount of food and don't maintain a healthy body weight. That's my fault. Sometimes it's because it's a reaction to the drugs I am on, or I may over-eat as a reaction to stress, a lack of self-discipline, or just because I enjoy what I am eating! My biggest weakness is apple pie and Scottish tablet.

One way of helping us look at our diet and make some appropriate changes if need be is to keep a food diary for a week. If we record everything that we eat, we will almost certainly be surprised at what we eat and when. A food diary may help to identify the times when we tend to snack and will help us to be prepared. Instead of rushing to the shop to buy a packet of sweets, we can have a few good options ready so that we can replace a naughty snack with a healthy one.

Healthy eating is especially important when we are in the

middle of a crisis or when we are coping with chronic illness. A healthy diet and even the addition of extra nutrients or vitamins (on sound medical advice) will boost our immunity and help us to be more resilient.

Sleep

When we talk about sleep we need to consider that it's not just quantity that matters – it's also the quality of sleep. How we sleep can impact how we feel throughout the day. To ensure we have a good night's sleep and are rested for the day ahead we need to consider our sleep schedule, bedtime habits, and our day-to-day lifestyle choices, such as how much caffeine we consume.

It is important to support our body's natural rhythms. We all have a natural rhythm of activity and rest. In the biblical story of creation there was night and day, emphasizing the key role of rest. It is therefore essential to understand our natural sleep-wake cycle or circadian rhythm. (As we will see in the next chapter, sleep is not the same as rest.)

A circadian rhythm is any biological 24-hour rhythm sustained and driven by a circadian clock – the word "circadian" comes from the Latin words *circa* meaning "about", and *dies* meaning "day". Our circadian clock is found in the brain, in the hypothalamus gland, which regulates most of the important functions of the body. In the hypothalamus gland the suprachiasmatic nucleus (SCN) cells receive information about light and dark via our eyes. They help us to process whether it is day or night, leading to the production of the hormone melatonin, which peaks at night.

If this cycle is disrupted there can be some negative short-term effects, as I experienced recently when I travelled home to the UK from Uganda. The condition is commonly called jet lag. Symptoms can range from fatigue and disorientation to insomnia. It is therefore important to try to go to sleep at a similar time each day. Sticking to the same time will help our body utilize its circadian clock and optimize our sleep. This means we should try not to nap after meals, but instead find something to stimulate us until the blood flow to our internal organs returns to normal after eating. Napping can be helpful if we need to recharge our batteries after lost sleep but should not be a regular habit. A fifteen- to twenty-minute nap should be enough to recharge us in the afternoon.

As we have seen, melatonin is controlled by light exposure and helps regulate our sleep-wake cycle. It is secreted more when it's dark and causes us to become sleepy. When going to sleep we should minimize our exposure to light and ensure we do not spend all our time in an environment with unnatural light (this includes mobile phone screens or computers). It is also helpful to reduce any stimulants that disrupt our sleep-wake cycle, the chief culprits being caffeine or alcohol.

Any of us who have experienced insomnia or a fitful night's sleep will understand how this can impact our resilience. Speak to any night-shift worker or nursing mother. We should value the eight hours of sleep we have each night because a good night's sleep will often prepare us for the challenges of the day ahead.

A theology of physical fitness and well-being

There is a theology of physical fitness and well-being that is birthed out of 1 Corinthians 6:19–20 (NRSV):

> Or do you not know that your body is a temple of the Holy Spirit within you, which you have from God, and that you are not your own? For you were bought with a price; therefore glorify God in your body.

In today's society, in which obesity has reached epidemic proportions, I would certainly suggest that this goes hand in hand with self-discipline. I am aware that when I am well enough to exercise regularly I feel more disciplined and able to take on more challenges. Other areas of my life – my prayer life, for example – come under control. I enjoy swimming although my respiratory problem has meant that I have not been able to do this for a while. In the past, while I was lane swimming, I would pray for one person for every length I swam. In 2011 I did a sponsored swim for breast cancer research and managed to swim sixty lengths. I prayed during that time and was really blessed through it.

In the sequel to *Tom Brown's School Days*, called *Tom Brown at Oxford*, the author Thomas Hughes reminds us that "a man's body is given him to be trained and brought into subjection". It can then be used for God's work in proclaiming the gospel. Certainly, throughout the history of the church, God's people have recognized the benefits of physical activity and sport – self-discipline, teamwork, and physical well-being, to name but a few. Pope Pius X declared: "Young people should perform physical exercises. Performed in moderation they will not only promote the health of the body, but also the salvation of the soul."[12] Interestingly, Pius X was pope at the time of the Christmas Eve truce in 1914 when German and British soldiers declared an unofficial ceasefire to strains of "Silent Night", playing football in no man's land between the opposing lines of trenches. Football was initially frowned upon by the Puritans who associated it with gambling and drinking, and yet many current UK Premier League clubs (for example, Aston Villa, Tottenham Hotspur, Liverpool, and Everton) were established by local churches for their youth groups.

We have discussed that there are ways we can prepare to run the course we are called to. These methods can help us improve our physical resilience. As a nurse I would also recommend that we have a yearly "well man" or "well woman" check. (Going back to the illustration of the car – most cars have to have an annual MOT and it would seem sensible that we too have an annual check-up.) I would also stress the need to attend regular screening. I have spoken with missionaries working overseas who do not have any routine screening done; they believe God will look after them because they are working for Him. Of course, we are all called to give our lives in service to God. Our responsibility is to ensure that we keep fit and well and this does not diminish, regardless of whether we are in East Africa or Europe. There is often a local capability for delivery of screening services. Some health organizations will provide virtual records and reminders for annual testing. The tests can be done locally and results sent to the external health providers who will interpret them for the client. Technology such as Telehealth, which allows clinicians and patients to communicate, despite being physically apart, has revolutionized health care.

So how did I respond to those missionaries? I challenged them, suggesting that it is their responsibility to ensure they keep fit and healthy. And that challenge is the same for me. I may deal with a long-term condition on a daily basis but I know I can be more proactive in keeping well. This will support my resilience when bad news comes my way.

We need to take care of ourselves. No matter how low we get or how much we feel challenged by life, we need to eat, drink, exercise, and rest. And my friend who decided to climb a mountain? I heard today that she reached the summit of Mount Kilimanjaro. Maybe she was more resilient than we thought she was!

PRAYER

Dear Lord,

Thank You that You are our Creator God.

Forgive us when we are not as disciplined as we should be. We can make wrong decisions about our timetables, what we eat, or when we sleep. Help us to use our bodies for Your glory. Help us to be wise with what we do with the bodies You have created for us. Empower us to live for You.

In Jesus' name,

Amen.

CHAPTER 4

Rest

Having four small children under five-and-a-half years old was a challenging time for us. While the experience was an amazing blessing it was also extremely tiring. In fact, it was more than that: Malcolm and I lived in a fog of eating, drinking, work, and very little sleep. Our four children had a different sleep-wake rhythm than we did. Physically, it felt like we were wading through treacle. And any woman in the early stages of pregnancy will know how that feels. I am sure I had conversations with people and agreed to all manner of things that I really cannot recall (and for that I apologize!).

The lack of sleep, coupled with constantly being on the go physically, inevitably left us mentally exhausted at times and not as sharp as we should have been.

Have you ever felt that exhausted? Maybe you have had to leave what you loved doing to rest a while? Sometimes we need someone to tell us to rest. I know Jesus did. In Mark 6:31 Jesus said to the disciples: "let's take a break and get a little rest." The verse, in *The Message*, continues, "For there was constant coming and going. They didn't even have time to eat." The disciples had just been commissioned and were on the road to sharing the amazing news about Jesus.

People were being healed in body, mind, and spirit, and the disciples were witnessing astounding miracles as people were set free. Would you want to stop? "Let's take a break and get a little rest." I would want to keep going, but Jesus knew the disciples needed to rest and be reminded of where their strength came from.

Mark 4:35–41 shows us that Jesus has the ability to rest during a crisis when He and the disciples are caught in a storm.

What would you do in the middle of a storm? My mind goes into overdrive when we are in crisis and I confess that rest is not the first thing I think of.

Storms. My own experience of being caught in a bad storm on a ferry in the middle of the English Channel impacts my choice of films. I hate any films about snow and water. The snow one is obvious – who wants to feel cold? Not my idea of fun. Water, however, is a different matter.

When I was about five my parents and I were coming back to the UK for a short time from being stationed in Germany. We were all in one cabin trying to sleep as one of the worst storms of the year battered our ferry. In the end we had to drop anchor and wait for the storm to pass. Mum was trying to keep my baby sister happy as Dad held on to my brother and me. Our cabin had a tiny sink and we were all terribly seasick. Feeling sick, being sick, and also feeling scared meant that we could not sleep. We were definitely not resting! Could you?

In the story in Mark 4, Jesus and the disciples were clearly not on a ferry crossing the English Channel, where boats like the P&O *Spirit of Britain* carry around 1,000 cars and 2,000 passengers at a time, and have all manner of in-built safety features to cope with the worst excesses of the sea and weather. That particular boat is a massive 700 feet long and 100 feet wide.

Instead, Jesus and his disciples were probably in a small open fishing boat. As he crossed the Sea of Galilee, a furious storm suddenly hit the boat from out of nowhere. These experienced fishermen had not foreseen such a violent storm. They were in the middle of the largest freshwater lake in Israel, the source of which was the River Jordan. Sudden storms were common due to the lake's low situation in the Jordan Rift Valley. By the time Jesus was on the boat there would have been about 200 small fishing boats on the water trying to make a living from tilapia and other freshwater fish. Today, this large body of water is the source of most of Israel's drinking water.

The disciples were experienced fishermen in a storm on a large lake and they were scared. They were not trying to make a living – they were just trying to live. Would you simply sit back and close your eyes in that situation? Would you be able to lie back in your bunk and sleep? That is exactly what Jesus did. He knew that He could rest in any storm. It is a reminder to us that we need to rest.

The definition of rest

The Merriam-Webster dictionary defines "rest" as "a bodily state characterized by minimal functional and metabolic activities".[1] Rest can therefore be defined as the ability to stop work or activity to relax or sleep.

When we think of the word "rest" we associate it with others in the same semantic field: relax, lounge about, flop, pause, time-out, peace, stop, sleep. These are often passive words reminding us of inactivity. However, rest in itself is not passive.

In sport, a distinction is made between active and passive rest. Passive rest means doing nothing – no training whatsoever. At the very most, it might be a brisk walk but that's it. In contrast, active rest involves the sportsperson doing a workout that is of reduced intensity. A cyclist may just go on a shorter-than-usual 45-minute ride. This is very helpful for training and is called "recovery" as the athlete's body is given time to recover from days of intense exercise.

Active recovery or active rest focuses on completing an exercise programme at a low intensity. At the same time, however, it is intense enough to speed up the blood flow around the body, so enhancing the clearance/elimination of waste products and the enzymes responsible for muscle damage and residual fatigue. In summary, the person is still exercising, allowing their heart to pump faster, speeding up the waste elimination process from the cells or allowing them to re-synthesize proteins that have become damaged.[2] In the same way there should be a change of pace in all areas of body, soul, and mind.

The difference between rest and work is the *intention* of doing the exercise.

Maria Popova writes about listening to Rhesa Storms, a preacher at the Forefront Church in New York, who challenged Popova about the theology of rest. In her Brainpickings blog, Popova quotes Storms as follows:

> *We're picking up cues from our culture about the way we live our lives and the pace at which we*

live our lives. Rest isn't a priority, because so often rest is confused with laziness... Sometimes, rest isn't a priority because we've incorrectly measured success... Rest, instead of being something passive, is actually an act of resistance. We live in The City That Never Sleeps — so resting may be the most countercultural and spiritual thing we do with our lives.[3]

The definition of sleep

The Oxford English Dictionary defines sleep as "a condition of body and mind which typically recurs for several hours every night, in which the nervous system is inactive, the eyes closed, the postural muscles relaxed, and consciousness practically suspended".[4]

As humans we usually spend a third of our lives asleep. That's equivalent to one hour of sleep for every two hours we are awake.

There are two main stages in normal sleep patterns. These are: 1) rapid eye movement (REM) sleep, which is the period when the brain is active and the body does not move; 2) non-rapid eye movement (NREM) sleep, when the brain is less active but our body can move.

For a "normal young adult", 20–25 per cent of sleep time is REM sleep. As we age, we need less sleep, particularly after we turn sixty. Culturally, we also have one period of sleep although the circadian rhythm of sleepiness is actually biphasic and we all experience afternoon drowsiness between about 1 and 3 p.m. – perfectly in time for school finishing! Do I hear the word "siesta"?

When we sleep our brain does not work actively as we don't have to use our full consciousness. This means that our brains as well as our bodies can rest. When we rest, however, we relax our body for a while but we still use our brains, for example, when we are sitting on the sofa reading a book.

Why do we rest and sleep?

We all have a natural rhythm. The German chronobiologist Till Roenneberg suggests that we all possess an internal timing mechanism that regulates our own unique sleep pattern. We have an internal circadian biological clock that is controlled by the suprachiasmatic nucleus found in the hypothalamus in the brain. It responds to dark and light and therefore regulates our sleep and wakefulness. When it is light, cells in the optic nerve in the eye are stimulated, sending messages to the hypothalamus. Our body temperature rises, levels of the cortisol hormone increase, and we wake up. Melatonin is the hormone produced in the evening that makes us feel sleepy.

Our rhythm also shows some variation throughout the day. As I mentioned above, our strongest need to sleep is between 1 and 3 p.m. and also between 2 and 4 a.m. This is also dependent on a wide range of different factors, one of which is age. We all know about the toddler who wakes up at 5 a.m. or the adolescent who trundles downstairs in the late morning or early afternoon for breakfast!

Roenneberg believes that we should not stigmatize people who are early or late risers because they already have cultural challenges. Consider the seventeen-year-old studying for his A-levels, having to be in lessons at 8.30 a.m. His internal time pattern cannot be altered simply by going to bed early – this is something that takes time to adjust. Perhaps as a society we should consider starting lessons later!

In one private school in Surrey in the UK, the start time of lessons has been changed to 1.30 p.m. instead of 9 a.m. The decision to do this was based on the work of Professor Francesco Cappuccio of the University of Warwick, an expert in sleep.[5] He proposes that teenagers have a delayed phase clock – sleeping later and waking later.

God has a rhythm, a pattern, and this is clearly seen during creation. God looked at what He had created at the end of each day in the creation narrative. He created a world with rhythm. In God's world we breathe in and out twelve to twenty times a minute, and our hearts beat 60 to 100 times a minute. Through the recurring seasons, and across the weeks and months and years, the twenty-four hours in each day change in a rhythmic pattern from day into night.

The word "rhythm" comes from a Greek root meaning "flow" or "stream". It is the essential element in music, and it reflects the pattern of everyday life. The first thing each of us heard in the womb was the continuous rhythm of the woman who carried us – a continuous rhythm of rest and activity.

Speaking about rest, Peter Knight, a gifted musician and friend of mine, said that "every piece of music begins and ends with silence". Music inherently depends on silence to allow us to hear the notes that are played, to distinguish the melodies, and hear the rhythm. It also gives us time to reflect on the music. Bach used silence in his St Matthew Passion. Listen to Handel's Hallelujah Chorus and rest and reflect in the silence.

And in art? I recently asked another friend, Stephen, why we need to rest. He replied: "Like an artist standing back from the canvas, a rest enables us to regain the whole or bigger picture and in so doing be re-inspired to continue."

It also reminds us that we need God, that we cannot achieve everything in our own strength. It is a reminder that as Christians we are not self-sufficient. In the creation narrative God rested at the end of each day. He is God – He doesn't need to rest but He set us an example, a spiritual discipline.

We need to keep in time with God's rhythm: "And evening passed and morning came" (Genesis 1:5, NLT). And on the seventh day He rested. He wants rest to be a part of our day because rest is part of God's rhythm for us.

The physiological reasons why we sleep

There are a variety of physiological reasons why we need to rest and sleep but the process of sleep is one of the least understood human biological activities. The ancient Greeks understood it as the time when the brain fills with blood that drains away before we wake and refresh it. We know we need to sleep to allow our brain to process new information and commit it to memory. Sleep also removes all the junk and stuff we don't need to remember. This process is called memory consolidation. The body also uses sleep to send in its own rubbish collectors to retrieve and eliminate any cellular waste (that is, the waste produced by our neurones during wakefulness). We also know that a good night's sleep can improve our ability to concentrate and learn.

Sleep also enables carbohydrates to be broken down and stored, regulating the hormones that are needed to help us grow and develop. If we don't get the sleep we need over a prolonged period of time our risk of weight gain can increase. This is because the hormone levels that affect our appetite and how we process sugars and carbohydrates are changed. So for every hour we don't sleep, our risk of developing obesity increases.

Sleep is also needed to support our cardiovascular health. Our heart is a muscle and when we sleep it is able to slow down and increase any cellular repair processes. Lack of sleep can lead to hypertension and irregular heartbeats as the heart is unable to rest.

Not only this, but sleep also enables our bodies to fight disease more effectively and enhances the action of the immune system. Lymphocytes, T-cells, and Th cells travel between the blood and lymphatic system while we are awake. At night these cells migrate to the lymph nodes, ready for action if our bodily defences are attacked.

Our body can cope for a single night without sleep and is not unduly stressed by this. It is a period of continuous wakefulness rather than sleep deprivation. It is the longer periods without sleep that cause negative impacts on our bodies, and it is unclear how long we can survive without sleep. In 1965 Randy Gardner, a sixteen-year-old San Diego high school student, tried to break the world record for the longest time spent awake. During the course of the experiment he developed problems with his eyesight as well as speech and memory problems. Toward the end he also started to hallucinate and eventually had to stop the experiment on the eleventh day.[6]

Why we don't sleep

There are three main types of sleep disorder: trouble staying awake, trouble sleeping or insomnia, and abnormal behaviour during sleep. The majority of people with sleep disorder have insomnia or have trouble sleeping. There are a variety of reasons why we can develop these sleep disorders, and it is helpful to try to identify the physiological or psychological factors that can interfere with sleep.

There are certain things that can alter our sleep patterns. Significant noise, such as aircraft passing, can raise adrenaline and noradrenaline levels, an effect which is detrimental to achieving recuperative sleep. Travelling also disrupts sleep, especially jet lag when we travel across several time zones. This can upset our biological or circadian rhythms.

Some medications can alter our sleep pattern. Anyone having problems with sleep should check with their GP that they are not using medication such as decongestants or steroids, and some medicines for high blood pressure, asthma, or depression can also cause sleeping difficulties as a side-effect.

Caffeine is the most popular drug in the world and occurs in the coffee bean, tea leaf, kola nut, and cacao pod. It is, however, a stimulant, and is even given in drug-form for premature babies to stimulate their slow heartbeat. It may help keep us awake by stopping the action of sleep-inducing chemicals but it cannot replace sleep.

Anxiety and stress can lead to sleep-onset delay or psychophysiological insomnia. I can certainly relate to this. If I am concerned or worried about something I can lie awake for hours thinking about it, causing me not to be able to fall asleep. I have had to learn some relaxation techniques to help me; one of my strategies is to recite Scripture, particularly the psalms. (Try reading Psalm 91:11: "Whoever dwells in the shelter of the Most High will rest in the shadow of the Almighty" and Psalm 121:3: "He will not let your foot slip – he who watches over you will not slumber.") If we have chronic sleep deprivation we have a greater tendency to fall asleep during the day, even at work, and we are more likely to make mistakes (for example, medical errors, road traffic accidents, and life-changing accidents with machinery). It's estimated that lack of sleep is a major contributory factor in some 100,000 road-traffic accidents each year in the USA. Lack of sleep can also change our mood, making us more irritable, moody, and impatient.

Here are some interesting facts and figures about sleep:

- There are over seventy different types of sleep disorder.

- 60 per cent of adults complain that they have at least two disturbed sleeps a week.

- We need an average of eight hours' sleep a night.

- Humans are the only animal that can decide not to rest when they need to.

- Our bodies **never** adjust to shift work.[7]

When things go wrong

Lack of sleep can have disastrous consequences. In 2013, Moritz Erhardt, a 21-year-old German man, died before reaching the end of a seven-week internship at the Bank of America in London. He collapsed and died in his home after working until 6 a.m. for three days in a row.[8]

The Japanese word *karōshi* is defined as "death from overwork". The first reported instance occurred in 1969 when a 29-year-old man employed in the newspaper industry died of a stroke due to lack of sleep. A few years later, in 1974, the German-American psychologist Herbert Freudenberger wrote about "burnout", defining it as "physical or mental collapse caused by overwork or stress"; in the 1980s burnout became a recognized cause of death. Nowadays, each year, hundreds of overworked Japanese men and women die from heart attacks, strokes, or suicide (the Japanese word for suicide due to work stress is *karojisatsu*) – again, brought about by a lack of sleep. And according to a recent report from Australia, it is typical in the financial industry for people to work an eighty-hour week (thirteen-hour days for six days a week, finishing at 11 p.m. every night).[9]

In 2000 the WHO produced a report about the worldwide issues surrounding mental health and work, concluding,

> Employers have tended to take the view that work and/or the workplace are not etiological factors in mental health problems. However, whatever the causal factors, the prevalence of mental health problems in employees makes mental health a pressing issue in its own right.[10]

Since publication of this report, governments have tried to ensure that strategies are in place to support employees. This includes working with employers to identify vulnerable workers and encouraging a healthy work-life balance. We need to ensure we have downtime to recover from the stresses our bodies and minds go through at work. But of course, on the other hand, some people tip the scales in the other direction and spend too much time focusing on leisure activities.

A press report from 2015 told the story of a 24-year-old Chinese man who died after playing *World of Warcraft* for nineteen hours without rest.[11] Incredibly, another gamer, a Taiwanese man from New Taipei City, died and was left undisturbed for nine hours in an internet café after suffering a cardiac arrest while at his machine. And in 2011 a 20-year-old British man, Chris Staniforth – who would typically play his console for twelve hours at a time – died from a pulmonary embolism after a prolonged session on his Xbox. These facts and figures obviously remind us of issues around gaming addiction but also of the imperative to strike a balance between work and rest.

Why we don't rest

So why don't we rest when we should? Let's look at the theology of idleness.

A theology of idleness

Idleness and leisure are well known to have been the goals of ancient Greek culture.[12] Aristotle, for example, asserted: "This is the main question, with what activity one's leisure is filled." I wonder, however, if we don't quite give the ancient Greeks the credit they deserve. Perhaps their idea of leisure included time to study and reflect on life. The Greek word for leisure (σχολη, *skholé*) gave rise to the Latin word *scola* – from which we derive our English words "school" and "scholar". Leisure was long considered to be the basis of culture – that was until this view was challenged by the theologian, Bernard of Clairvaux (1090–1153). He was a French monastic reformer who supported the Cluniac order, personally overseeing the building of sixty-five new monasteries, supporting the establishment of 300 Cistercian monasteries, and establishing the Cistercian Order. A dynamic individual, he was sought on many occasions to counsel important leaders of the day and was involved in reconciliation between France and England. He wrote about the importance of work and a theology of idleness. Throughout the Middle Ages the concept of idleness challenged people to work because work was the reason for their existence: this argument was justified on the basis of Scriptures such as Proverbs 18:9, Proverbs 20:13, Proverbs 21:25, and Proverbs 24:30–34.

In 1972, the year after the word "workaholic" was first coined by the American psychologist Wayne Oates, the German philosopher Josef Pieper challenged the view that the goal of human existence is just work.[13]

In the 1930s the writer and philosopher Bertrand Russell recalled being brought up in a generation that considered idleness as a characteristic of the devil, whereas a strong work ethic was considered a virtue:

> I want to say in all seriousness, that a great deal of harm is being done in the modern world by belief in the virtuousness of work, and that the road to happiness and prosperity lies in the organized diminution of work.[14]

He stressed the importance of enjoying rest and leisure and that good morality and a good nature flowed out of this rather than out of work.

As Christians we are aware that our morality and right choices flow out of a desire to follow Christ and live in His strength. In fact, we could argue that making good choices and living a Christian life flow out of resting in God and His strength. Too often, however, we fill our days with other things because we think it is counter-cultural simply to be at rest. Rest is not made a priority because it is still viewed as idleness and confused with laziness.

We also live in a culture that does not sleep. Technology has made life harder rather than easier because we cannot switch off. We can check our emails while we are munching our breakfast, on our journeys to work, and in our lunch breaks while we sit at our desks with our sandwiches. I have often sat in a restaurant and watched couples sitting together, eating together and texting, Facebooking or emailing – *but not together*. Peter Kreeft, a Christian and a professor of philosophy at Boston College and at the King's College (Empire State Building) in New York City, suggests that time is a casualty of computer technology because we have less free time, not more.[15]

I wonder if we don't stop because we are fearful to stop. If we stop we have time to think and reflect and therefore have no option other than to confront the negative aspects of our lives.

Why we should rest

Let's look at a biblical perspective as to why we should rest.

A theology of rest

God has given us a theology of rest, known as Sabbath. This was given to us in the creation narrative. The principle was also handed down in the Mosaic Law in the fourth commandment ("Remember the Sabbath day by keeping it holy" – Exodus 20:8). Sinclair Ferguson, the Scottish Reformed theologian, suggests that humankind was commanded *to rest*. This means ceasing from everyday work and spending time with God. He also highlights the need to stop being self-sufficient and to rest in God's grace.[16]

We are reminded that since Jesus died and rose again, we have eternal rest if we trust in Him. But we are not there yet! We are reminded of the eternal hope we have when we observe the guidance around Sabbath and rest. In fact, Ferguson calls Sabbath "Father's Day", a reminder of the one with whom we are spending time.

The Jewish Sabbath started in the evening: in the creation narrative we are told that "evening passed and morning came" (Genesis 1:5, NLT) – a reminder that our day starts in the evening as we rest in the knowledge that God is with us and is sustaining us.

There are arguments about whether Sabbath is a twelve-hour or a 24-hour period. There is even confusion about when it starts and ends in the Arctic Circle, where, at certain times of the year, there is no night. Whatever the details, the principle we should follow is that we are to make rest a ritual.

Jesus observed it (Luke 4:16) and so did Paul (Acts 13:42–44). We are made in God's image and as His children we should include rest in our rhythm of life as Jesus and Paul did and as Hebrews 4:1–13 expounds. God wants us to rest, to delight in Him, in each other, and in the circumstances of our lives.

The Old Testament scholar, Walter Brueggemann, writes: "Sabbath is the cornerstone of faithful freedom."[17] Sabbath rest is an act of resistance against the culture of the day. It may be counter-cultural to stop and rest but there is strength when we do. Until the mid-1960s the Soviet State encouraged a six-day working week. Communist China only began to observe the two-day Saturday–Sunday weekend on 1 May 1995. Rest was not considered to be something important.

Initially it may be strange to slow down and take time out. It may feel uncomfortable. It goes against the flow and the prevailing cultural norms. In fact, we are called to be different from the people around us (Matthew 5:14–16). Rest should be part of the rhythm of our lives. During periods when we personally have been really busy, God has made us stop on numerous occasions. You would think we would learn!

As with the physiological process of sleep, we need rest times to heal us and to remove the debris from our minds. We all need to learn to be dependent on our Maker to restore us.

When I think about rest and stillness and what the Bible has to say on the subject, I find myself drawn to Psalm 46. In the opening verses the psalmist reminds himself that God is "our refuge and strength". And this abiding truth remains, even though the earth may give way and the mountains fall into the sea; even though the nations may be in uproar.

Then, in verse 10, he hears God calling him to be still in the midst of life: "Be still, and know that I am God." Like the psalmist, we should continually remind ourselves that we are not God and realize that it is in the stillness that we get to know Him. As *The Message* version states: "Step out of the traffic! Take a long, loving look at me, your High God, above politics, above everything" (Psalm 46:10).

Jesus also reminds us of this key principle: "Come to me, all of you who are weary and carry heavy burdens, and I will give you rest" (Matthew 11:28, NLT).

How can we practically rest?

There are certain things we can do to help us rest. One strategy is to recognize whether we are an early riser or a late riser and understand what our natural rhythm is. Once we have identified our rhythm, we can then plan our day around those patterns.

I am a natural early riser so on days when I write I am often up, already sitting at my laptop by 7 a.m.. I also need an afternoon rest and so I do not fill my late afternoons: at 3 p.m. on my days off I am often found resting on the sofa!

Plan to rest and put it in the diary.

Malcolm is one of the busiest people I know – and he plans ahead. All birthdays and special days are ring-fenced in his diary years ahead. We book his holidays in his diary well in advance. If we know we have a period of time when we are particularly busy in ministry, we ensure we have a few days off after the event to rest and spend time with the One who strengthens us.

Also, family time doesn't necessarily count as Sabbath

time or rest. I am not saying that family time is not important. What I am saying is that time with God is more important.

We also need to remember to be present in the moment and to use the time we have efficiently. When I am standing doing the dishes I focus my mind and think of my Saviour. Susanna Wesley – the mother of John and Charles – was married for forty-four years. During that time she experienced illness, disease, terrible poverty, two house fires, and the death of nine of her nineteen children. Being "busy" as we understand it today is such a lame concept that does not even begin to capture her world. As a committed Christian, Susanna gained her strength from her God. When she wanted time out from the business of her home she would often sit with an apron on her head – reminding her family she was focusing her time in prayer and meditation with God. He was the one who gave her strength for each day. We need to learn how to have such "apron moments" in the busy-ness of our days.

According to author and theologian Tim Keller, "Rest, ironically, is an activity that must be prepared for and then pursued."[18]

PRAYER

Lord, thank You that You show us the need to rest, the need to actively take time out from the busyness of the day.

Thank You that You remind us that Your rest is enough to get us through days when we feel exhausted and have no more strength. Help us to stop long enough to think about You. Thank You that You remind us that we need to rest and be strengthened by You.

Help us to make this the rhythm of our lives.

Please help us to learn to be in Your presence.

Amen.

Increasing Our Mental Resilience

CHAPTER 5

How Can We Increase Our Mental Resilience?

There are certain words or terms that make us switch off when we hear them because we don't think they apply to us. Mental illness is one of those terms – it is something we don't talk about. There is stigma attached to it and there are also wrong health beliefs. We may think it does not apply to us, but what we do know is that worldwide figures show that mental health afflictions are on the increase. Depression is currently the fifth cause of disability in the world and is projected to jump to second place by 2020.[1] Although there are a range of treatment options such as medication and counselling, prevention is the best option.

This chapter will look at mental health, well-being and resilience, and how we can prevent mental illness.

We all have mental health. Some of us are in better mental health than others, just as some of us are in better physical health than others. We may define "mental health" as our emotional well-being or our thoughts and feelings about ourselves and others. Keeping good mental health means we can make the most of our lives and manage the ups and downs we face with resilience.[2]

The Bible teaches us how to live a life that supports mental resilience. That can be a little surprising, as, on the surface, a lot of the passages we read tend to emphasize how it is important not to be anxious or fearful. Here are just a few of those verses:

- "Do not be anxious about anything, but in everything by prayer and supplication with thanksgiving let your requests be made known to God. And the peace of God, which surpasses all understanding, will guard your hearts and your minds in Christ Jesus" (Philippians 4:6–7, ESV).

- "Cast all your anxiety on him, because he cares for you" (1 Peter 5:7).

- "Peace I leave with you; my peace I give to you. Not as the world gives do I give to you. Let not your hearts be troubled, neither let them be afraid" (John 14:27, ESV).

- "The waters closed in over me to take my life; the deep surrounded me; weeds were wrapped about my head at the roots of the mountains. I went down to the land whose bars closed upon me forever; yet you brought up my life from the pit, O Lord my God. When my life was fainting away, I remembered the Lord, and my prayer came to you, into your holy temple" (Jonah 2:5–7, ESV).

- "For God gave us a spirit not of fear but of power and love and self-control" (2 Timothy 1:7).

THE ART OF DAILY RESILIENCE

- "Therefore do not be anxious about tomorrow, for tomorrow will be anxious for itself. Sufficient for the day is its own trouble" (Matthew 6:34).

- "Fear not, for I am with you; be not dismayed, for I am your God; I will strengthen you, I will help you, I will uphold you with my righteous right hand" (Isaiah 41:10).

In fact there are at least 500 verses alone about fear in the New International Version (NIV) of the Bible. The Bible is therefore clearly the place to turn when we need to be encouraged during tough times. It is the place to be built up in faith and mental resilience for when the difficult times come.

The Bible also provides clear guidance on how to live. Dig a little deeper and we can learn lessons that support our mental resilience. We all know people who appear to be more positive than others. Certainly new experiences and supportive relationships create physiological changes in the brain structure. It is obvious that optimism and resilience can be developed when we are a part of a supportive community. The Christian community is one of God's great gifts to us. Sharing and supporting each other means we move from isolation and negativity to positivity and purpose. And all we are doing is simply sharing life together.

Living in community

1. Hebrews 10:24–25 says,

   And let us consider how to stir up one another to love and good works, not neglecting to meet together, as

> *is the habit of some, but encouraging one another,*
> *and all the more as you see the Day drawing near.*

2. Acts 2:42–47 says,

> *And they devoted themselves to the apostles'*
> *teaching and the fellowship, to the breaking*
> *of bread and the prayers. And awe came upon*
> *every soul, and many wonders and signs were*
> *being done through the apostles. And all who*
> *believed were together and had all things in*
> *common. And they were selling their possessions*
> *and belongings and distributing the proceeds to*
> *all, as any had need. And day by day, attending*
> *the temple together and breaking bread in their*
> *homes, they received their food with glad and*
> *generous hearts...*

Louis Cozolino, the author of the 2006 best-selling book, *The Neuroscience of Human Relationships*,[3] writes about how relationships build our brains, suggesting that there is an emphasis on individualism. He also suggests that we need to help form the prefrontal cortex of the brain through healthy early relationships. This allows us to trust others, control our emotions, and maintain a positive outlook. Froma Walsh, a professor of both social services administration and psychiatry at the University of Chicago, agrees with this. In her 2006 book *Strengthening Family Resilience*,[4] she suggests that resilience is an ongoing interaction between nature and nurture, encouraged by supportive relationships.

We are also taught to be honest and transparent with God. We need a realistic view of our strengths and weaknesses.

With such self-awareness we can turn to God, conscious of our own weakness, and request His help. When we fail, we pick ourselves up, fall at the Cross, and ask Him for His help.

There are so many characters in the Bible that show us how we can be like this. One of my favourite books is the Psalms, where the writers pour out their heart to God. They are so truthful about their lives but at the end of each psalm they have a positive sense of realism. There is a sense of reality rooted in the kind of thinking that views adversity as something we have to walk through. Without that sense of belief that things will change, we don't have the mental resilience to believe things will improve.

We want to utilize tools that will enhance our spiritual and emotional well-being and develop strategies for resilience training, such as positive psychology. Positive psychology is a fairly new field of study that takes a holistic approach to a person's well-being – one that emphasizes the importance of spiritual well-being.[5]

It was an approach that was founded by people such as the American psychologist B. F. Skinner who, in the 1960s, put forward the proposition that behaviour could be influenced through the use of positive and negative reinforcements. Abraham Maslow, in the 1970s, followed Skinner's work with studies on the positive potential of human growth. He suggested that an individual's highest need is the ability to self-actualize or to maximize their personal strengths.

Positive thinking

We have seen above that positive thinking can help our mental resilience. In Philippians 4:8 the Bible tells us what

82

is proper thinking: "And now, my friends, all that is true, all that is noble, all that is just and pure, all that is lovable and gracious, whatever is excellent and admirable—fill all your thoughts with these things"(NEB). A tall order, but if we consistently apply these positive words it will help us develop positive thinking – a habit that is crucial to the stability of our mental health. If we fill our minds all the time with negative and destructive thoughts from the world around us they will have a negative impact on us.

Years ago one of my children became addicted to a British soap opera called *Eastenders*. Every episode was a drama of pain and destruction. It has been suggested that the script editor, Tony Holland, wrote it this way not only to cover many controversial issues from society at the time, but also to make us appreciate our own lives more! It took a while but we soon realized that our child became very miserable and grumpy after watching the programme. It really affected his mood! It is important for us to eat a healthy diet or we fall ill. We need to feed a mind to keep it healthy. Paul reminded the Christians in Philippi to fill our minds with truths – those things that are good and deserve praise; things that are true, noble, right, pure, lovely, and honourable.

Just like a physical health check, there are also a variety of methods we can use to measure our own mental health. By doing so we can identify areas that need to be strengthened. We can use tools such as questionnaires to measure our well-being, and review how well we are feeling and functioning in everyday life.

One such tool is the Warwick-Edinburgh Mental Well-being Scale (WEMWBS), available online at http://www.nhs.uk/Tools/Documents/Wellbeing%20self-assessment.

htm. Its scale consists of fourteen positively worded statements, each with five response categories. A score in the range from 0 to 32 points indicates very low well-being, while at the opposite end of the spectrum a score of 59 to 70 points indicates above average well-being. The website also provides suggestions for further action, depending on the score. The Mental Health Foundation notes that people completing a questionnaire often detect an improvement when they re-evaluate their mental health three months later. If we use the WEMWBS we should ensure that we follow the guidance once we have worked out our final score. Where there is concern about our well-being, we should involve our loved ones and invite them to walk the journey of improvement with us.

Craig Groeschel, the founder and senior pastor of Life. Church, Oklahoma, in his book *Soul Detox* suggests that toxic influences and attitudes do affect us.[6] He advises we go on a detox, identifying things in our mind that badly affect us, such as lies, negativity, or wrong thinking. He suggests that we replace these lies with biblical truths and the healing positive words of Jesus. It may not be quite the same as colonic irrigation but it does mean washing out all the rubbish that has piled up in our mind.

Resistance is not resilience

Often the words resistance and resilience are linked together, although they do not mean the same thing.

Resistance can have a negative impact on our mental health. It is a term I vaguely remember hearing about during my school days while learning about physics – not my favourite topic (I don't think anyone in our family did well in our O Level or GCSE physics)! I have to confess that I did have to look it up again to make sure I had the right terminology. It is, in fact, the ability of something not to be affected by something else, and it is not the same as resilience.

In physics, resistance is represented by the letter "R"; it is the opposition that something offers to a flow of electricity or electric current, for example. It is the opposite of conductance, which is a measure of the ease with which electrical current flows through a substance.

I want to look at it here as often we think we are being resilient when actually we are just being resistant to what God wants to say. In short, resistance is the friction that can occur in an electrical circuit preventing the flow of the current. We think we are standing firm when actually all we are doing is causing friction and not allowing God's Spirit to move in our lives.

There are three levels of resistance to change:

- **Level 1:** Resistance is due to a lack of information or confusion about key information.

- **Level 2:** Resistance is an emotional reaction to the proposed change due to fear of loss (for example, of the status quo, position, salary, and so on).

- **Level 3:** Resistance is based on what the change represents to the individual. This may be deeply affected by the individual's personal, cultural, religious, or racial differences and experiences.

Recognizing where we are in this process can help us change. This can also help identify strategies to help us cope with future change. When we become a Christian we are complete in Christ but we are also changed on a continuous basis to be more like Him. Let's remember to ask God if we think we are stuck in any of these levels. He will help us to move on. Identifying where we are resistant may in turn help us improve our resilience.

As Christians we can become resistant to God's voice if we don't always listen to Him. After a while, living our own way, we become resistant to what He is telling us. This is certainly the case for persistent wrong behaviour. However, God loves us and does not give up on us that easily. As with the children of Israel, He constantly calls our name.

Actively keeping our minds healthy

There are a number of strategies we can employ to keep our minds healthy and we will look at some of these in more detail in later chapters. But for now, it will be helpful to reflect on the following:

Accept that you are unique and special to God. His love is limitless and unending. His Son died for you so that you can have an intimate relationship with Him.

Remember you have hope – hope that reminds us that you are not defined by your illness.

We are made in the image of our Creator God. It is therefore good to foster creativity, and this comes in all manner of forms. Start a new hobby, start new relationships, experience the life you are a part of, and challenge your mind to think about new ideas and concepts.

Use your mind as a muscle: try to problem-solve simple tasks alone – or team up with someone else because we were made to be in community.

Generate good disciplines such as meditation and mindfulness. Feed your mind on the right diet: watch what you ingest in the same way as eating a healthy diet with plenty of fruit and vegetables.

Find time to get rid of the waste. Confront problems, solve problems, and get rid of negative thoughts: replace them with positive thoughts. Take time to memorize Scripture.

Embrace simplicity – don't over-complicate things that can generate stress.

Finally, talk to others who share your life and who know you well.

PRAYER

Father God,

Thank You that we are fearfully and wonderfully made. We are so aware that we consist of body, soul, and mind. We find it difficult to comprehend how these elements operate and the intricate ways they link up and work together. Sometimes we are not aware of how things work in unison until one area does not function as it was intended to. This is often the case with our minds – our mental well-being.

Help us to have strategies in place to keep our minds active and healthy. Help us to be able to love and support those who experience illness in this area. We need Your wisdom. We know as a church that we often fail You. Help us to be an inclusive community, loving those who may feel stigmatized by the world.

In Your Son's name,

Amen.

CHAPTER 6

Fear and Anxiety – That Unknown Place

We have all experienced anxiety and fear – whether in the form of hiding behind the sofa as we are watching Dr Who fight the Daleks or waiting for our driving test to start, not knowing what traffic conditions we might encounter and how we might cope.

As previously mentioned, the Bible mentions fear over 500 times. Other phrases such as "fear not" are also present in the Bible. The King James Version includes twenty-nine instances of the phrase "be not afraid". In fact there are 365 derivatives of "do not fear" in the Bible – one for every day of the year. If it is mentioned so many times then surely God is telling us that at some point we will be fearful; we will get anxious.

So in this chapter we will examine what fear and anxiety are and examine how they affect us. In particular, we will consider fear of the unknown – a variety of fear that can grip us like a vice, leaving us feeling bruised, squashed, and damaged. The psychological feelings of anxiety and fear are very real: they can cloud our thinking and make us irrational, and they can also adversely affect our mental resilience. How can we deal with these feelings and prevent them from impacting us in such a dramatic way?

The words "anxiety" and "fear" are often used together in the same sentence – and sometimes the terms can be interchangeable. Fear can be defined as a state of body and mind that develops in response to a specific stimulus that leads to reactive behaviour. We are afraid – and we run from the cause of our fear. As we grow up we are reminded of situations or circumstances that have frightened us in the past, and we learn to avoid repeating the same situation. We all know that we should not head to the basement in the dark if we hear noises down there. It's a scary scenario and all the movies we have seen prime us to expect bad things: the torch is dropped, the battery fails, or the lights go out and we head downstairs to impending doom.

However, fear may just as easily relate to something that we have never experienced before. We might be going into a place or situation we know nothing about and we feel as though we cannot "get our head around it".

According to the American horror writer, H. P. Lovecraft (1890–1937): "The oldest and strongest emotion of mankind is fear, and the oldest and strongest kind of fear is fear of the unknown."[1] Psychologists call this fear of the unknown "xenophobia", a term that is derived from the Greek roots χενος (xenos), which means "foreigner" or "strange" and φοβος (phobos), which means "fear". It therefore refers to an irrational sensation of fear related to people or environments that are perceived as strange or foreign. It is the sensation of fear of the unknown – something we often experience when we are out of our comfort zone.

Not everyone reacts in the same way and we respond differently to different threats, whether perceived or real. Some people bounce back from trauma while others need longer to process what has happened. We know that although there is variability in how we react or respond to fear, our recovery often relates to our background. There are categories of people who generally cope better than others when they are put in frightening environments. Because it is not easy to gain ethics approval for a study that involves scaring people, it can be difficult to research fear responses in humans. That is why much current research into fear has been done on animals – of course, ensuring full compliance with animal welfare legislation.[2]

Research in rats has shown there are different phenotypes of responders to fear.[3] In the light of this work our response to fear is now believed to be far more primal than was originally thought.[4] Our subconscious often takes over when we are afraid. When we are exposed to a fear-inducing stimulus our automatic response is one that we have learned by association. We are scared so we call for help. For example, if we are scared of drowning, we are reminded of what other people have done and so we wave our arms and shout. In Matthew 14:22–33 Peter looked down, became afraid, and called for help as he tried to walk to Jesus across the Sea of Galilee. He had already got out of the boat; he had even taken some steps. He knew that Jesus was the Son of God and had seen Jesus walking on water. But he allowed his subconscious nature to take over from his intellect and his heart – after all he was a fisherman. He was afraid that he might drown as he was literally in deep water.

Behavioural psychologists would agree that there is an animal fear response that is more complicated than "fight or flight". You may have heard about this while at school in those boring biology lessons! As we saw earlier, the fight or flight response is a well-known phenomenon. Hormones help the body to prepare for immediate evasive action. These are just a few of the immediate responses: there is huge increase in blood flow to the muscles, a release of energy from the cells to aid the muscles, and muscle tension increases to give muscle strength and support immediate evasive activity.

Although anxiety is associated with fear, it is a different entity. They may be associated together but anxiety differs from fear by being defined as a psychological, physiological, and behavioural state. This behavioural state can be triggered when there is a threat to a person's well-being. Often this may be as simple as a degree of uncertainty about something. When someone is anxious, physiological changes occur in our bodies. These are manageable in specific limited episodes when we are anxious for a short time. However, chronic or pathological anxiety interferes with our ability to cope with life's challenges. Anxiety and fear are therefore thought to function as triggers for these adaptive biological responses. While some believe that they are the same as they both elicit a warning response,[5] others contend that they differ in how they develop and present, in the pattern of response and their intensity.[6] Anxiety has also been described as:

> *a unique and coherent cognitive-affective structure within our defensive and motivational*

system. At the heart of this structure is a sense of uncontrollability focused largely on possible future threats, danger, or other upcoming potentially negative events, in contrast to fear, where the danger is present and imminent.[7]

Anxiety is therefore considered far more as a generalized response to an unknown threat or internal conflict, whereas fear is more focused on a specific danger or an actual threat.[8] We know that fear and anxiety lead to a range of adaptive or defensive behaviours that help us escape from the source of danger or motivational conflict.[9] Whether we believe that we have evolved the fear-mediated response of fight or flight or we believe that God birthed it in us, it has a positive purpose. We are, however, vulnerable to the physiological and mental effects of prolonged anxiety. In short, prolonged anxiety can have a negative affect on our bodies.

The prolonged effects of anxiety and fear

Living with constant fear and anxiety can lead to a range of different health issues, from gastrointestinal problems such as irritable bowel syndrome (IBS) through to long-term fatigue, reduced fertility, and quite significant cardiovascular events. Being dominated by fear and anxiety can also weaken our immune system, making us more susceptible to a range of illness.

About 15 per cent of the population of the UK suffer from IBS,[10] a condition in which the nerves regulating digestion are hypersensitive to triggers such as anxiety and stress. The symptoms of abdominal pain, bloating, fatigue, and altered bowel habit can be genuinely debilitating.

The immune system is a complex network of cells and organs that defend the body against infection. A normal healthy immune system remains in homeostasis – or balance – but prolonged anxiety and stress cause the cells and organs that compose the nervous system to release hormones that trigger the production of white blood cells. Usually these cells and other mediators help us fight infection but it is detrimental if this over-production continues for more than a short period of time. Chronic over-stimulation of the immune system causes it eventually to become suppressed and we are unable to fight off disease and infections. We can all think of people who have ended up struggling with nasty colds or chest infections when they are studying for exams.

People with high anxiety levels are also 59 per cent more likely to have a cardiovascular event than those with normal anxiety levels. High levels of anxiety significantly increase a person's risk of developing heart disease and of suffering a fatal cardiac event.[11] High anxiety levels are believed to be a stronger risk factor for cardiovascular problems than even smoking and high blood pressure!

Prolonged fear can also have a significant impact on our psychological well-being as it can damage the formation of long-term memories. We find it difficult to regulate the normal fear response and end up living in a world governed by fear. Our ability to regulate emotions, communicate, read non-verbal cues, reflect on our actions, and even to act ethically can be affected. Our emotions become intensified and a law unto themselves.

Is there something we can do?

A few years ago Malcolm and I both changed jobs, and moved house and church. There were new schools for our four children and a new community to explore – what you might call exciting times. Everything was new and we loved getting to know our amazing church family. However, within a year of moving I had a bad bout of pneumonia, exacerbated by asthma and persistent breathlessness. My exercise capacity dwindled from attending the gym three times a week or doing a sixty-length sponsored swim to being unable to walk up and down the road to our local shops. I felt that God took me to an unknown place: it was scary, frustrating, and exhausting, both physically and mentally. Thankfully I recovered sufficiently after a few months and headed back into the daily pattern of life and work.

One day I was praying about what had happened because I was still not back to full health, and I was wondering if I would have the energy and resilience I had had before. I felt that God answered my prayers and I was left with the thought that things were going to get worse before they got better – and they did!

Within the year I was back in that scary unknown place. I was diagnosed with methicillin-resistant staphylococcus aureus (MRSA) infection in my lungs and with brittle asthma. It took a further three years before I had the all-clear although my lung function still shows some residual damage. At the time, however, I had no idea if things were going to get better or not. I simply had to trust God that He had promised me that things would get better. I cannot say that I leapt out of bed every day singing hallelujah and trusting God; in all honesty there were days when I forgot His promise to me. I felt things had just got worse and I wondered whether I would ever have a month without a bout of bronchitis or a chest infection. Would I always feel this fatigued? The crunch time came when I was heading to work on the London Underground and fell asleep. This was more than my usual Tube-induced nap, and when I woke up I did not know if I was heading home or going to work. I was grateful to my family for spurring me on, reinforced by close friends who supported and encouraged me. Through them I was reminded of God's promises to me.

I am not claiming that now I have it all sorted, because I don't. Next time I find myself in a place I don't know, I'm not sure how I will react. But I *do* know that God was with me last time and helped me through it, and He's still with me now as I adapt to new rhythms and patterns in my life.

God also reminds us in His word that other people have had to face their fear of the unknown. In Hebrews 11:8 we read that God called Abraham to a place he had not travelled to before: "By faith Abraham, when called to go to a place he would later receive as his inheritance, obeyed and went, even though he did not know where he was going." And when I think of what the apostle Paul coped with, I am as "blown away" figuratively as he was physically.

The "unknown place" in the title of this chapter can be a physical location or a period of change in our lives when we face challenges we have not faced before, such as illness, job loss, or bereavement. God wants us to hold on to His promises and trust Him because He is with us on every step of the journey.

No easy answer

There is no easy answer to some of the challenges that arise when anxiety and fear impact our lives. Phobias, acute anxiety syndromes, and chronic anxiety may develop due to a range or combination of genetic, physiological, and psychological factors. However, there are some things we can learn that will keep us focused and enable us to feel there is some control in our lives.

The most profound and yet simple thing we can do is to recognize when we are becoming anxious, to identify the triggers, and turn to Jesus. Focusing our mind on Him will help in ways we cannot comprehend. We come to realize that we are not floundering in a storm but that someone is steering and guiding us out of this unknown place. Jesus says to us: "Come to me, all you who are weary and burdened, and I will give you rest" (Matthew 11:28).

The Message helpfully paraphrases these familiar words in verses 28–30:

> Are you tired? Worn out? Burned out on religion?
> Come to me. Get away with me and you'll recover
> your life. I'll show you how to take a real rest. Walk
> with me and work with me – watch how I do it.
> Learn the unforced rhythms of grace. I won't lay
> anything heavy or ill-fitting on you. Keep company
> with me and you'll learn to live freely and lightly.

Sometimes we need just a few minutes to focus on God before we enter a potentially fearful situation. Stand still, take a deep breath, and focus on something that centres your mind and thinking on Him. This may involve looking at the trees outside or experiencing the solid physical sensation as our fingers touch something in God's natural world. In that moment we are intentionally remembering that the One who created us is here with us. He gives us strength.

I am reminded too that the psalmists regularly use this principle of centring their mind on God despite all they are going through. As we read, we walk with them through their own list of awful circumstances – from privation to disappointment to loneliness to war – before affirming with them *"and yet* 'I will rejoice in the Lord',[12] *and yet* 'I will say of the Lord'[13]… 'my hope is in you, [O Lord]'".[14]

You can develop skills that help you become more resilient, able to face future challenges in a positive way. These are some examples:

- be a part of a church family, a community of God

- stay accountable to the church family – allow them to point out any wrong behaviour

- be able to identify when things are starting to go wrong

- develop strategies you can use if you become over-anxious

- ask God for wisdom and that His Spirit will highlight wrong behaviour

- set realistic goals in behaviour modification

- remember you are not alone: you do not have to do this by yourself.

Reproduced here as paraphrased in *The Message* version, Paul's instructions in Philippians 4:6–7 are wonderfully applicable:

*Don't fret or worry. Instead of worrying, pray.
Let petitions and praises shape your worries
into prayers, letting God know your concerns.
Before you know it, a sense of God's wholeness,
everything coming together for good, will come
and settle you down. It's wonderful what happens
when Christ displaces worry at the centre of your
life.*

PRAYER

Dear Lord,

*There are days when we don't trust You as we should.
The anxieties and worry of life take over even though
You tell us not to worry. Help us to take a deep breath
and to learn to focus on You in these moments. You are
our centre. Help us to keep returning to You.*

*And for those people who suffer significant illness in
the area of anxiety and fear we ask that You intervene
in a supernatural way. Give them Your peace and
grant them Your strength to cope with their everyday
challenges.*

In Jesus' name,

Amen.

CHAPTER 7

Mental Health, Mental Illness

For years we were not open about talking about mental health or mental illness within a church setting. I don't know about your experience but mine is that it was never really discussed. The only sermon I ever heard about it was at a youth event when the preacher spoke about Jonah and told us that he was depressed. It stayed with me through the years. For me, it made Jonah's character feel so real, so colourful, so relevant. If we were depressed, wouldn't we also hide from the world? Maybe not under a tree, but certainly in a quiet place!

Despite the fact that we are only just beginning to talk about mental illness there are some dramatic facts about it that may be surprising to you. According to Mind, the UK mental health charity, one in every four people will experience a mental health condition this year.[1] One in every three GP practice consultations is related to mental illness.[2] One in seventeen people lives with a significant mental illness such as bipolar disorder or psychosis.[3] Another more concerning fact is that 17 in every 100 people have suicidal thoughts.[4]

Only yesterday we were at a church conference where Malcolm shared his personal story. A lady in her late seventies or early eighties approached us, unable to talk. She was gulping for breath as she tried to tell us that her son had died fourteen years ago. He had taken his own life. She shared her story as if it had just happened. The pain of loss and grief streaming down her face mixed with confusion and hurt as to why he had to end his own life was obvious. How do we help people who walk this walk?

And then there are the facts that most mental health conditions such as schizophrenia and bipolar disorder are present by the age of fourteen years. One in ten children experiences mental illness related to self-image, bullying and/or cyber-bullying, abuse, or social stress.[5] This means that most of us have come across people who have had some sort of mental illness or we ourselves have suffered from it. We don't live in isolation when we are members of a church: we are a community and what impacts us in the world outside impacts us inside the church too. Mental illness affects us as believers no matter how old we are and we are not very good at supporting people who live with it. We are far better at caring for someone who has an acute physical illness by weighing in with offers of cleaning, lifts, or cooking spaghetti bolognese, shepherd's pie, lasagne, or other comfort food. (Once when Malcolm was in hospital with meningitis, seven different well-wishers spontaneously – but without comparing notes – delivered spaghetti bolognese to us on seven consecutive days!)

When I was fourteen I was introduced to Jesus for the first time. The person who told me about Him became my best friend at school. She was a very talented musician and top of her class in many subjects. But by the time I was sixteen I could barely recognize my friend as her behaviour became increasingly erratic. I did not know that she was presenting with symptoms of schizophrenia.

Her parents finally asked me about her behaviour and I was very distressed at having to talk about my friend in that way. I felt it was somehow my fault that she was eventually detained under the 1983 Mental Health Act in the UK and received treatment in a psychiatric hospital. I did not understand what had happened or even know much about her illness. Over the years she has been in and out of hospital but has always needed institutional support. I remember visiting her in my first year at university and feeling that I had let her down, not praying for her enough. It would have helped me if I had understood something about mental illness from an early age.

If many of these disorders first present in early teens then educating young people about them will enable them to care effectively for their friends. Why don't we talk about these issues in youth groups or even in our Sunday services? In this chapter we are going to look at what mental illness is, how we can support people living with it, and how can we improve our own mental health and well-being.

What is mental illness?

The Merriam-Webster dictionary defines mental illness as:

> *any of a broad range of medical conditions (such as major depression, schizophrenia, obsessive compulsive disorder, or panic disorder) that are marked primarily by sufficient disorganization of personality, mind, or emotions to impair*

normal psychological functioning and cause
marked distress or disability and that are
typically associated with a disruption in normal
thinking, feeling, mood, behaviour, interpersonal
interactions, or daily functioning.[6]

Mental illness is therefore a condition that impacts a person's ability to think, feel, or carry out the activities of daily living. The cause of the illness is not always known but may be related to traumatic experiences, genetics, drug and alcohol abuse, developmental and social factors, and underlying physiological changes in the brain and nervous system.

While we have not identified the causes of most mental disorders we are aware that many non-psychological factors play a role. One example might be a person's genetic make-up, which can increase their risk of developing a psychotic disorder. Looking at this the "other way round" we are reminded that psychological factors such as stress are also associated with increased susceptibility to physical illness. We may not always know the exact causal pathway of the illness (what medical people call its "aetiology") but we have an understanding that there are psychological factors involved.

The difficulty about how we define mental illness is that even within the psychiatric field different approaches are used. The medical model is the most common method of diagnosing and treating a patient who has behavioural problems. However, values have to be assigned to what is "normal" and what is "abnormal" and these can vary from culture to culture. Writing in 1992, Jerome Wakefield, a professor of psychiatry in the USA, claimed that not all dysfunctions are disorders or illnesses.[7] He suggested that our society may have changed so much since the times when our characters were formed that even if a person lacks certain abilities it does not mean they have a disorder. He concluded that mental dysfunction therefore is an illness or disorder when it causes harm to the person or others.

It is no surprise, then, that we find it hard to define mental illness. Perhaps our focus should be on the whole person and their well-being rather than what is physically or mentally wrong with them? How should we respond to people who appear to be living with mental illness? We also need to focus on how we can strengthen our own resilience so that if our own mental health is affected we can cope better. Perhaps there are ways we can actively keep our minds healthy.

Personal experience

As mentioned in Chapter 2, in 1990 I experienced a period of clinical depression after a broken engagement and other personal issues. There were no other causative factors when I developed my mental illness, and the people in my church did not know how to respond. I loved them, they were my church family, but I could not explain how I really felt. I think they just thought I was a little down. In reality I felt lost, alone, and in a deep pit of sadness that I could not climb out of. There were some days I just wanted the sadness to end. I did consider suicide and I think that's why this issue resonates with me so much. I can understand why people want their days to end. There is no condemnation here from me. Regrettably I would not have been able to tell people in my fellowship about how I was feeling without feeling even more of a failure. I felt they would have simply told me to stop feeling sorry for myself. Every time I tried to get out of the pit I slipped back down into the mess below. What I needed was someone to stretch out their arms to help me as I climbed out of that pit of depression.

Thankfully an amazing person called Julia accepted my struggles and was there for me. She would call round unexpectedly and drag me out to the cinema or a theatre. She did not make me feel less of a Christian because I had these struggles. Mercifully, the episode lasted only nine months but it birthed in me an understanding of how mental illness impacts people and how they can feel like second-class citizens in the church.

Almost 10 per cent of the population will have had at least one major depressive episode in the past year.[8] Often, as my episode was, it will have been related to a significant event. However, it is more than just a period of sadness or a rough patch. Depression is a serious mental health condition that can lead to devastating consequences for patients and their families. It is an illness that impacts all races, ethnic backgrounds, and socio-economic groups. Although it's a common illness, at the time I felt I was the only one suffering with it, and that no one understood. I felt isolated from the world around me. I was certainly unaware that mental illness could impact my own life. I was aware of other strategies to keep my body and spirit healthy but no one had ever mentioned the importance of keeping a healthy mind.

I want to digress for a few moments. I want to explore why we have ignored mental health and illness within the church setting.

Mental illness and the church

Historically, the church played a vital role in supporting people who were being made whole and in the healing of mental illness through religious practice.[9] This formed an important element of early church life. Part of the problem was that mental illness was not viewed as a medical issue: abnormal behaviour was instead thought to be caused by demonic possession, a view held by the cult of Asclepius in particular, which believed in supernatural solutions to mental illnesses.

During the fifth century BC this cult co-existed with the Greek philosophy of Hippocratic medicine (based on observation, logical deduction, and experimentation) and – centuries later – with Christianity, confusing people further by giving them an even more fractured picture of the philosophy of health and illness.

The philosophical views embodied in Hippocratic medicine eventually gained the upper hand and generally came to be accepted by the church as it sought to treat the body and care for the mind. In Europe, by the advent of the Middle Ages, schools of thought began to emerge where there was a glimmer of understanding that people could suffer with mental illness in much the same way as they could with a physical ailment. In fact, it was an early thirteenth-century Christian monk called Bartholomeus Anglicus (Bartholomew the Englishman) who first proposed music as a potential remedy for people suffering from depression.

Over the following centuries, long before the establishment of the UK's NHS in 1948, the church helped to fund and build hospitals for the "insane" to care for and treat such patients. While some of the more barbaric treatment methods should rightly be questioned, it is important to remember that their efforts marked the first stumbling attempts to move out of centuries of ignorance about such matters and forward into a more enlightened approach encompassing new methods such as counselling and psychology.

It is also strange to think that throughout the history of the church many well-known Christians (including Augustine, Ignatius of Loyola, Charles Spurgeon, C. S. Lewis, Mother Teresa and Martin Luther King Jr) have struggled with mental illness. Nevertheless, despite such well-documented high-profile cases, the church's response to mental illness is not as advanced or as sympathetic as it might be. The worst of sins was considered to be suicide: a taboo topic not to be discussed. For some, this notion has not changed. Hopefully our understanding of just how devastating mental illness that leads to suicidal thoughts or indeed suicide itself can be for a family has grown.

Interestingly, in modern times, anthropologists have found that in non-Western cultures not all mental pathology is viewed as an illness; some instances are related to other causes, for example, a trance-like state due to demonic possession, rather than what would be credited, in Western cultures, to schizophrenia.[10] Certainly this is an area where we need to expand our knowledge because the prevailing confusion has led to those with mental illness being labelled and treated as if they are stigmatized.

The social stigma of mental illness

Stigma is regarded as a sign of disgrace or has negative connotations that can cause individuals to be set apart or isolated. The stigma is related to the individual's unusual behaviour or their personal experience. The concept of stigma was highlighted in Erving Goffman's seminal book first published in 1963[11] and since then extensive research has been done in this field.

When questioned, people with mental illness describe stigma amounting to their being ashamed that they have the condition, leading to their feeling isolated or excluded. Many individuals feel that in suffering from mental health issues they are labelled with shame as they adopt society's views about them and their illness.[12] I have spoken to people with mental illness who have been led to believe that they "are not strong enough" or have a "weak character". I have even spoken to sufferers in church communities who believe that their illness and symptoms are due to their lack of faith or spirituality.

Nine out of ten people with mental illness will experience stigma, a complex concept that is divided into three main categories. Perceived **public stigma** is the belief that people with mental illness are stigmatized by society; **personal stigma** refers to our individual beliefs about mental illness; and **self-stigma** is the individual's view of their own mental illness.[13] These beliefs are related to our own experience of mental illness and knowledge and education.

The stigma of mental illness can be as harmful to the person as the symptoms of the disease. It can lead to marriage breakdown, discrimination, unemployment, and social rejection.[14] Patients may themselves not seek help due to the perceived stigma of diagnosis and disease. They may not take the medication they are prescribed due to wrong health beliefs and stigma.[15] This brings us to something we can do to help: we can help break down these barriers of stigma within the church environment and in our local communities. Let's challenge our own preconceived ideas of mental illness and consider what it means to the sufferer and their families.

Lack of understanding

It is shocking to realize that stigma and a lack of understanding about mental illness remain common problems. Even today, the church still does not always cope well with people who are experiencing mental illness. It is often presumed that the individuals concerned are engaged in a spiritual struggle that causes mental and emotional strain; as such they may simply be branded as attention-seekers who disturb the Sunday services. People who experience issues related to alcohol or drug addiction are sometimes blamed for their own conditions. And how do their families cope?

In 2012 a family in David Murray's congregation at Grand Rapids Free Reformed Church in Michigan, USA, donated a large sum of money to facilitate research into mental illness and the church. The donor family had struggled for many years with relatives living with mental illness. In 2014 LifeWay Research published its initial findings on this topic, highlighting that approximately 66 per cent of pastors do not speak to their congregation about mental illness.[16] Report author, Bob Smietana, revealed that only a quarter of churches know how to respond when someone is diagnosed with mental illness. Few churches with a counselling service have a counsellor who is experienced in mental illness or knows someone who can help.

But surely, as Christians, we want to help sufferers of mental illness? It is important to know how people feel. How does their illness impact them and how can we as a loving community support them? An understanding of mental illness and transparency about people's experience can help us as we actively seek ways we can improve our own resilience in this area.

Writing online in *Relevant* magazine, Andrea Jongbloed openly discusses how she felt when she was diagnosed with bipolar disorder at thirteen years of age.[17] Her church and friends were very supportive, particularly as they had known her before her illness. However, when she visited other churches she found that the reception she got was very different. Describing what happened when her symptoms became apparent, she noted that, "fear gripped those Christians, so they over-reacted". Showing profoundly perceptive insight, she comments that the church's fear comes from a place of lack of understanding. We need more people like Andrea who are prepared to talk openly about their illness to a non-judgmental audience.

Patients with mental illness – and their families – have to cope with the social stigma around their illnesses. It is a terrible indictment that they sometimes also experience this stigma in their church family. Amy Simpson has this to say in her excellent book about mental illness and the church: "Our shame and abandonment are the last things people affected by such illness need."[18] She suggests that we have a tendency to reduce people who are mentally ill to caricatures or ghosts and simply refuse to talk about the subject. Instead of ignoring the issue, let's challenge ourselves to facilitate a conversation.

The opposite of being ignored is being made the centre of attention. For some reason as Christians we feel a need to **shout loudly** about some topics. Mental illness is one where the chant can be: "You don't need medication or psychiatrists to treat your depression; there is deliverance and healing in the Word of God." My response to this is that yes, God gives us all we need but He has blessed us with the medical profession; I would not be a part of that profession if I didn't believe in what it has to offer. Pregnant women expect midwives to care for them in labour, parents of sick children hope that there will be a paediatrician on hand who can help, and patients with mental illness also need help from the medical profession.

Let's have an open dialogue about mental illness. After all, one out of four of you reading this book will experience it. So let's:

- identify the signs of mental illness – can we recognize the signs and symptoms in our families or ourselves?

- learn about the associated costs of mental illness from stigma to the financial costs of long-term sick leave or unemployment

- understand and learn about the treatment options.

Treatment options

Today there exists a wide range of treatment options available for patients with mental illness. While we may well have stereotypical ideas about electroconvulsive therapy (ECT) and antipsychotic drugs that sedate people, there are other more modern approaches to treatment, such as cognitive behavioural therapy ,that can make a real difference in the lives of patients living with mental illness.

Problems can occur when people are encouraged to stop taking their medication and to trust God only for healing – advice that is given more often than we might think. Again, according to the LifeWay Research report quoted earlier, only 40 per cent of pastors in the USA believe that medication helps in cases of acute mental illness. Stanford's survey of 293 participants with mental illness found that 30 per cent had had a negative interaction with the church.[19] What is more, women were found to be significantly more likely than men to have their mental illness dismissed by the church and/or be told not to take their psychiatric medication.

How can we help?

Like the man described in Ed Stetzer's *Christianity Today* article about mental illness,[20] I turned to the psalms. I think I realized that I could be honest with God just like David had been. I also struggled to find the words to use and I found that the psalmists' words met my need.

Let's share our experiences – perhaps they will help others. Let's talk to people and find out how we can help.

It is a sad truth that it takes the death of a prominent

figure for us to start talking about this topic. The tragic suicide due to depression of the talented actor and comedian Robin Williams in 2014 prompted any number of articles in the press. The same happened in the Christian press when Rick Warren, the senior pastor of Saddleback Church in the USA, lost his 27-year-old son Matthew to suicide after a long battle with depression.

Will van der Hart is pastoral chaplain at Holy Trinity Brompton in London and director of Mind and Soul, a Christian charity working to reduce the stigmatization of mental illness both within the church and wider society.[21] Will himself suffered from post-traumatic anxiety following the 7/7 bombings in London in 2005. He writes: "Different denominations have different attitudes, and some are further down the track than others, but I've still found in some congregations and traditions that there's a very simplistic and spiritualised view of mental health problems."[22] His take-home message is that, as churches, we have to stop stigmatizing people with mental illness and instead start loving them.

We also need to learn more effective communication skills because people with mental illnesses may be unpredictable and volatile and difficult to relate to. This can place us in a situation where we feel uneasy and don't know what to say. It is important to identify strategies that can help, get professional advice, and provide education in this area.

We can also pray for wisdom and ask God to show us what we can do to help and support the mentally ill. We are called to love them as we would our neighbour, believing the best of them and extending grace to them. We know too that the religious community can play a vital role in recovery from serious mental disorders.[23] So let's help people living with mental health issues to feel included rather than isolating or stigmatizing them – they have enough battles to fight in the world around them.

In summary, the LifeWay Research suggests that we:

- should improve our own education in this topic
- need to educate people of all ages about mental illness
- need to be able to recognize the signs of what to look for
- need to know how to respond if we suspect someone has a mental illness
- need to develop ways to be supportive without overwhelming the individual.

PRAYER

Dear Lord,

There is so much about the human body we don't understand. We are in awe at how You made us in an unique manner and in Your image.

Help us not to dismiss the things we don't understand and especially help us to love and care for those who have mental illness. Help us not to stigmatize people, label them, or make life difficult for them. Let our church families be living and inclusive, celebrating our differences and trying to make a difference in the lives of those who need it. Help us to learn to be kind and more like Jesus.

In Jesus' name,

Amen.

Increasing Our Spiritual Resilience

CHAPTER 8

How Can We Improve Our Spiritual Resilience?

While researching the topic of spiritual resilience I found an American website designed for people who were about to go on active service or were war veterans. One of the key messages was: "Increase your resilience"; it was stressing the importance of spiritual resilience. I was encouraged not only that the compilers had considered this, but also that they suggested meditation and prayer to a "higher power".

In its own research on resilience, the United States Air Force (USAF) has also acknowledged that improving resilience means that its military personnel and families were less likely to develop depression, anxiety, insomnia, substance abuse, post-traumatic stress disorder (PTSD), and suicidal thoughts.[1] The report authors emphasize that resilience needs to be increased in the physical, mental, *and* spiritual areas of people's lives. In the domain of spiritual resilience they argue that having beliefs or principles to adhere to helps people cope in difficult areas of duty, and that certain spiritual practices support spiritual well-being.

Hackney and Sanders' 2003 meta-analysis of religiosity and mental health found that there was an improvement in the mental health of patients if they maintained an element of personal devotion.[2] Similarly, Yeung and Martin suggest that spiritual practices such as meditation and mindfulness, prayer, or attending religious activities all have a distinct positive effect on well-being.[3] In this same area it has been shown that meditation can decrease stress and have a beneficial impact on the immune system.[4] Prayer has also been shown to help and alleviate the symptoms of people with anxiety and depression.[5] Similarly, praise and worship have been reported to have a positive effect on young people, improving their well-being and helping them feel connected to each other.[6]

The interesting conclusion to emerge from much of the above is that it is the *world* – and in particular, world of scientific research – that is telling us that we can improve our overall well-being if we follow religious practices, such as meditation, prayer, praise, and worship.

The spiritual disciplines

Spiritual disciplines are religious practices we can use that help us develop as Christians, thus enabling us to grow in spiritual maturity and resilience. The word "discipline" (same root as "disciple") is used because we need to train ourselves and allow God's Holy Spirit to change us in the process.

In the 1980s the Quaker theologian Richard Foster published *Celebration of Discipline: The Path to Spiritual Growth*, which outlines and discusses what he described as

117

the "twelve spiritual disciplines": meditation, prayer, fasting, study, simplicity, solitude, submission, service, confession, worship, guidance, and celebration.[7] The book heralded a resurgence of other titles reflecting interest in some of the well-known (but often ignored) disciplines of the Christian church. Foster suggests that using these practices not only helps us grow in our level of Christian maturity but also helps us develop a better balanced spiritual life. Not only are we changed by the *inward* disciplines of meditation, prayer, fasting, and study, but so is the world we live in by the *outward* disciplines of simplicity, solitude, submission, and service. And finally, the *corporate* disciplines of celebration, confession, guidance, and worship bring us nearer to one another, improving our sense of community, as well as drawing us closer to God.

Foster has since established a non-profit ecumenical organization in the USA called Renovaré (from the Latin word for "renewal").[8] The organization encourages the work of renewal of the church by concentrating on the "spiritual formation" of individual Christians and the use of these disciplines.

While we may not find ourselves in a military conflict zone, life can still be tough and we are definitely engaged in a spiritual battle, so we need all the armour we can use. I am going to focus on two of the spiritual disciplines listed above that can help us improve our spiritual resilience: meditation and prayer. These two disciplines are those that I found especially helpful when I was going through a particularly difficult time.

Meditation

Christian meditation has not always had good press. I sometimes wonder if this is because it is considered to be a universal practice associated with many of the world's major religions. However, Christian meditation is unique and distinct from these different types or styles of meditation (for example, as practised in Buddhism) because there is no suggestion that one should disengage the mind; instead it aims to fill the mind with thoughts of God or Scripture.

Christian meditation is actually rooted in the biblical text, being mentioned at least twenty times. Considered in simple terms, it can be defined as a form of prayer in which the person engages in a structured, intentional attempt to become aware of God and what He is saying.[9] Meditation comes from the Latin word *meditari*, which means to reflect on, to study and/or to practise. Christian meditation is therefore the process of deliberately focusing on God and His word.

According to Joshua 1:8 in the NIV:

> "Keep this Book of the Law always on your lips; meditate on it day and night, so that you may be careful to do everything written in it. Then you will be prosperous and successful."

The Message version puts it this way:

> And don't for a minute let this Book of The Revelation be out of mind. Ponder and meditate on it day and night, making sure you practice everything written in it. Then you'll get where

you're going; then you'll succeed. Haven't I
commanded you? Strength! Courage! Don't be
timid; don't get discouraged. God, your God, is
with you every step you take.

Psalm 1:2 (*The Message*) also highlights the importance of meditation: "Instead you thrill to God's Word, you chew on Scripture day and night. You're a tree replanted in Eden, bearing fresh fruit every month, never dropping a leaf, always in blossom."

Meditation has the same Latin word root as rumination. It's what a cow does when it chews the cud over and over in its mouth. In today's culture we invariably find it difficult to meditate. We struggle with the concept and with the practice. I know in the past when I have decided that I am going to spend some time meditating, I sit down with my Bible and then end up doing everything except meditate. My tummy rumbles, so I think about food; I hear a car outside and wonder when my car is due to be serviced. The list of distractions is never-ending.

In the 2015 movie *War Room*, the central character, Elizabeth, finds that her life is spiralling out of control. Her marriage is falling apart and she doesn't know what to do. Her work as an estate agent takes her to visit Miss Clara, whose house she has been asked to sell. Miss Clara is like a nuclear missile when it comes to prayer, and she encourages Elizabeth to pray for her family. Elizabeth clears her closet for prayer action (this is the "war room" of the film's title) but everything distracts her and she struggles to discipline herself simply to pray. She soon learns how to and the prayers of Elizabeth and Miss Clara begin to powerfully impact her family life. As I watched the film I had to laugh because I identify absolutely with Elizabeth – I'm good at finding things that distract me.

Meditation should be intentional: the words used to describe it (for example, "consider" or "ponder") carry the strong implication that people who meditate have taken time to clear space to think. The two Hebrew words for meditation are *haga* (to utter, groan, or ponder) and *sihach* (to muse, rehearse in one's mind, or contemplate).

Teresa of Avila (1515–82), the Spanish mystic and a Roman Catholic saint and reformer of the Carmelite Order, defined meditation in these words:

> By meditation I mean prolonged reasoning with the understanding, in this way. We begin by thinking of the favour which God bestowed upon us by giving us His only Son; and we do not stop there but proceed to consider the mysteries of His whole glorious life.[10]

Charles Spurgeon, the nineteenth-century theologian and preacher, highlighted the importance of reliance on God's Spirit:

> The Spirit has taught us in meditation to ponder its [the Bible's] message, to put aside, if we will, the responsibility of preparing the message we've got to give. Just trust God for that. But first meditate on it, quietly ponder it, let it sink deep into our souls.[11]

Influential commentators from all arms of the church suggest that meditation is a discipline we should participate in. We are therefore called to meditate on God and His word and allow His Spirit to speak to us.

Assuming that I am not alone in needing some structure to meditate, then the fourth-century Benedictine form of meditation called *lectio divina* (sacred reading) can be helpful. Traditionally a monastic tradition, it has become more popular in recent years. It adopts a very structured approach to meditation that is favoured by people such as Pope Benedict XVI and the biblical scholar, Eugene Peterson, best known for *The Message* transliteration of the Bible.

Lectio divina involves four stages. The first is *lectio*, which refers to the deliberate repeated reading of the same passage or verse of Scripture. The second stage is *meditatio* (discursive meditation) where the reader ponders the text. The third stage is *oratio* (effective prayer) where we pray to God and ask Him to reveal truths from His word through His Spirit. The final stage is *contemplatio* (contemplation) when we simply sit in God's presence, thinking about what He has told us. For myself, *lectio divina* is an encouraging process especially when reading the psalms. It doesn't matter which book of the Bible we read, the important thing is not to rush through huge passages of Scripture. Often just one single verse can sustain us for a long time. It can change how we are feeling and feed our souls.

Lectio divina also helps us change the naturally negative bent of our thoughts. We have anything between 12,000 and 60,000 thoughts a day and roughly 80 per cent of these are negative. We know that having positive thoughts leads to positive emotions, which can help improve our overall resilience.[12] Let's learn to swap those negative thoughts with positive promises from God's Word.

I wonder what would happen if we did that? Pastor Will Bowen of Christ Church Unity in Kansas City, Missouri, tried to help his congregation members find a way to stop complaining about their lives and instead focus on what was positive. One Sunday, in church, he gave them all purple bracelets as part of his "Complaint Free World Project". If they found they were complaining they had to change the bracelet to the other arm, helping them focus on changing their negative thought patterns. The Complaint Free World Project increased exponentially from 250 bracelets to five million bracelets in nine months![13]

Social psychologists tell us that it takes between eighteen and 224 days to change a behavioural trait, although in general the average time is twenty-one days.[14] Although it may take a little while to develop regular time to meditate on God's word, it is definitely worth it.

Prayer

The aforementioned movie *War Room* emphasizes the importance of prayer. As a spiritual discipline, prayer is something we recognize we should do – daily communing with the One who created us. I recently posed this question on Facebook: "If you believe in God, what stops you regularly having a set period of prayer each day?" Among the responses I received, one person suggested that the obstacle was the fluid pattern of her days because she has small children and a husband who works irregular hours. It is challenging when we don't have the supportive families around us that people may have had a generation ago. Some of my respondents mentioned lack of discipline, lack of time, or even giving it low priority. The crazy thing is that we know that prayer changes things: one person responded to my Facebook question and said that *nothing* should stop us.

I find it interesting that I am writing this on the very day that as a local church community we are opening the first 24/7 prayer room in our area. It is also the week that Christians around the UK are responding to the encouragement of the Archbishops of Canterbury and York to spend focused and dedicated time in prayer. The aim is that all Christians will deepen their relationship with Jesus so that we may have confidence in the future to share our faith and that all may respond to the call of Jesus Christ to follow Him.

These are exciting times! And who knows what will happen during or after the great wave of prayer between Ascension Day (5 May 2016) and Pentecost Sunday (15 May 2016)? It is brilliant that we are encouraged to be part of a national campaign to pray.

Prayer formed the subject of an Evangelical Alliance survey between 2011 and 2014.[15] The EA found that only 31 per cent of Christians set aside a substantial period of time each day to pray. 60 per cent of people responded that they prayed "on the move", with only 3 per cent struggling to pray at all. According to Richard Hansen and David Wall,[16] people don't pray for three main reasons, best summed up in the following questions:

- Will it work for me?
- Can I do it?
- What's it worth to me?

A daily prayer time and daily Bible reading were strongly recommended to me when I came to a living faith in Jesus. Friends trying to disciple me clearly showed me the importance of prayer, study, and meditation, and I am so grateful to them. In all honesty, I don't think I ever asked the last question: there was never a question about what I would gain from prayer. We don't talk to our friends because we wonder what it is worth to us; we talk to our friends because they are our friends. And so it is with prayer.

I have to confess that praying has sometimes felt like a chore, however. I do not jump out of bed at 6.30 a.m. every day singing "Morning has broken", shower, dress, clean the house, and have an hour praying on my knees. There have been days when I have not set time aside to pray because I have been caught up in the concerns of life. This is a bit like when we are feeling ill: we don't want to eat or drink but we know we need to have at least something. Our spiritual life is the same.

There are times when God seems far away although He is the same yesterday, today, and forever. In the EA study, 83 per cent of respondents had experienced a major period of difficulty in their life and God had carried them through it. During these times when we struggle to pray because our souls feel bruised and we are sick with anxiety or worry, we should take sips of His word. We should let Him know how we are feeling: Father, take this cup from me.

At heart, I wonder if we sometimes don't pray simply because we are overwhelmed with what is going on in our lives and we don't know what to say. I know that I have experienced times like that and yet I draw immeasurable comfort from God's intimately personal reminders in His

Word that He has made marvellous provision for us in such circumstances.

Paul encourages us in Romans 8:26–28 (RSV):

> Likewise the Spirit helps us in our weakness; for we do not know how to pray as we ought, but that very Spirit intercedes with sighs too deep for words. And God, who searches the heart, knows what is the mind of the Spirit, because the Spirit intercedes for the saints according to the will of God. We know that all things work together for good for those who love God, who are called according to his purpose.

Let's read those words again from *The Message*:

> Meanwhile, the moment we get tired in the waiting, God's Spirit is right alongside helping us along. If we don't know how or what to pray, it doesn't matter. He does our praying in and for us, making prayer out of our wordless sighs, our aching groans. He knows us far better than we know ourselves, knows our pregnant condition, and keeps us present before God. That's why we can be so sure that every detail in our lives of love for God is worked into something good.

I am so grateful that I serve a God who knows all about me – and who promises to be with me even though I don't always *feel* He is. A God who took on human form, who walked the walk, and knows what struggles we have.

So we pray because:

- God tells us to (Jeremiah 29:12–13; 1 Thessalonians 5:17; Ephesians 6:13)

- Jesus did it (Luke 11:1; John 17)

- Jesus showed us how and when to pray (Matthew 6:9–13)

- God reveals Himself to us through prayer (Psalm 143:10)

- He tells us He will help us carry our heavy load (Matthew 11:28)

- He listens to us (Matthew 6:8).

PRAYER

Dear Lord,

There can be a whole list of reasons why we don't pray or meditate on Your word. Help us to be honest and to learn from You. Help us to be dependent on Your Spirit who promises to utter the words we can't say. Let us be aware of Your presence with us. In moments when we don't feel anything, help us to stand firm on the promises in Your word, knowing you are constant and that You do not change – yesterday, today, forever.

Thank You for Your grace and mercy to us.

In Jesus' name,

Amen.

CHAPTER 9

Assessing Spiritual Growth/
Spiritual Health Checks

Last week I received a letter asking me to make an appointment for a health check at my local doctor's surgery. These health checks are offered to those in the UK aged forty and over. I have to confess I am now a few years over forty. The NHS health check looks at your cardiac health and the risk factors of developing long-term conditions such as diabetes or kidney disease. It's basically a midlife MOT. It is estimated by the Department of Health that these health checks can save up to 650 lives a year in the UK, prevent over 1,600 heart attacks, and identify 20,000 new cases of type 2 diabetes, which otherwise would have remained undiscovered until later in life.[1] Screening patients and identifying those at risk or in the early stages of disease means that future risks can be reduced and action taken to remove potential causes of ill health.

It's worth doing, even though I have been reminded that I am middle aged: appointment made for health screening.

I know some of you will wonder why I am telling you

this. I want to stress how important it is to attend for screening. Some of you will have had a regular health check done, some may have been screened for prostate cancer or even bowel cancer. Not all attend their primary care clinic for any form of screening as they just don't want to know what the results are or want to change any existing risky behaviour such as smoking or a poor diet. It is their choice and after all, it isn't particularly nice having a blood test or a smear test done. These can be embarrassing and sometimes a little painful.

We do know, however, that assessing our physical health has benefits despite the cost. Since we know that we consist of body, soul, and mind, I want to take this a little further: the question I want to ask is, how many of us have had a *spiritual health* check done? I asked exactly that question on Facebook a few weeks ago. I had no comments. No one I have spoken to has considered completing one. So why don't we do them? I think it's because they too can be embarrassing and even a little painful. I also think that in order to complete one successfully, we have to be self-aware. It is about the capacity we have to be open and honest about our strengths and weaknesses. To be self-aware means we possess a clear understanding of how we can impact other people and why we react the way we do in certain circumstances. We are in touch with how we think, what we do, and why we make the choices we do. The great sixteenth-century reformer, John Calvin, said in the introduction to his *Institutes of the Christian Religion*, "The knowledge of God and that of ourselves are connected. Without knowledge of self there is no knowledge of God. Without knowledge of God there is no knowledge of self."

Self-awareness

Self-awareness plays an important part in our growth as Christians. It is probably a key component of discipleship. Certainly Jesus is recorded as being exceptionally self-aware as He knew His role, His purpose, and where He was heading. So being self-aware, knowing who we are, and who made us is a wonderful blessing.

Being self-aware also means we can identify areas where there needs to be spiritual growth. I think most of us have some sense of awareness of our spiritual growth and our shortfalls. I know I allow the activities of everyday living to crowd my time and don't always allow space to spend time with God on my own. A spiritual health check means digging deeper into our lives. We need to be able to identify areas of spiritual deficiency and who wants to confess to that? It feels like such a personal thing, but confession of areas that we need to change is a good thing as it allows for more growth.

The psalmist said, "Search me, God, and know my heart; test me and know my anxious thoughts. See if there is any offensive way in me, and lead me in the way everlasting" (Psalm 139:23–24).

I want to add a cautionary note here. We know that there is a time and place for everything and doing a spiritual health check while in a period of stress or crisis is not a good idea. I think it will possibly add to the guilt that typically plagues Christians when life is hard and it is a struggle to cope. Instead I would suggest that this is something we can do when life is more stable and the path ahead looks straight. This exercise should not deflect from our moment-by-moment awareness of our total dependence on God and His Spirit. We want to grow more like Jesus day by day.

Spiritual health checks

Spiritual health checks are systems to help us identify any areas that we can improve in. It is not however a case of "do I pass the test or not?" None of us are perfect – I do not think we will all pass with flying colours. I certainly didn't, but it helped me identify areas I needed to work on. I am a sinner saved by grace living in a fractured world. I know God's Spirit can help me change – sometimes it's helpful to know where to start. We are saved by grace and called to grow in grace (2 Peter 3:18). So how and when do we do them?

When and how?

I think a spiritual health check is something we should do on an annual basis. Each year at work I have a personal development review (PDR); it helps me know what is going well, what areas need to change, and what areas I need support in. It also helps me and my manager identify the areas where I need further training and help, as well as helping me to develop in my role, pushing forward toward the goal. So a spiritual health check is also like a PDR and is best done individually but then discussed with your partner, someone you can be accountable to, or someone who is part of your church leadership. The key to it is that it is *intentional.* You are not filling a form in for the sheer fun of it: there is a reason for doing it. Involving someone you can trust means they can help you look at the areas you want to improve and develop strategies to do so.

There are several different tools you can use to do the health check. My suggestion is that you find one that works for you. This is not a "pat on the back" exercise. You want it to be robust enough to challenge you but easy enough to use that it is not something you struggle to do.

Many are simple forms that look at how we are developing in key areas such as:

* loving God

* loving others

* the spiritual disciplines

* prayer

* Scripture reading.

I want to focus on two tools I have found helpful but there are several others available online. It is a case of finding one that helps you the most.

The tools

The C. S. Lewis Institution annual spiritual health check[2] is based on Matthew 22:37–40 and suggests you look at two main commandments. The first is "Loving God with all your heart, soul and mind", with five questions asking you to look at topics such as, "How is my personal relationship with God?" or "Is there evidence of grace growing in my life?" The second section is titled "Loving your neighbour", involving ten questions such as, "Do we love our families as we should or is there someone we need to forgive?"

As you can see, they are challenging questions and you have to allow yourself time to reflect on them and consider your answers honestly. These are not tick-box exercises; rather they are tools not unlike our gardening apparatus, such as the spade, helping us to dig deep and to prepare the ground for new growth.

Trevor J. Partridge's health check for the Christian ministry Crusade for World Revival (CWR) asks respondents to fill in a form of thirty-five questions that relate to a scoring system.[3] A score of 35–49 reveals honesty and we are reminded that God will help us. A score of 175 suggests we are answering it in Heaven!

The CWR form contains questions that challenge and help us identify areas where we need God's help through His Spirit. The important thing to remember is that God can use this tool. It is not a questionnaire found in some magazine that we fill in for fun: it's a tool that can help us grow more like Jesus and that's exciting.

The score system helps us identify the discipline we struggle with and provides an opportunity to write an action plan for the year ahead with set objectives. In addition there are some exercises around forgiveness you may want to do, and some information about the spiritual disciplines to start you thinking about them. It is a comprehensive tool that is helpful to do and review with an accountability partner. Perhaps your partner can help you formulate achievable objectives that should be reviewed on a regular basis.

Health check questions

If you do not want to use one of the specified tools above then you could instead consider a few questions that may help you assess your spiritual health or well-being. I have aligned these to the areas we check in a physical examination.

1. Your vital signs: pulse, blood pressure, temperature. These are the normal signs that indicate that the body is functioning properly. In our Christian lives we can check whether we are having regular fellowship, reading our Bible, and praying.

2. Your height and weight: are your growing as you should? If you eat too much food you start putting on weight. If you don't correctly utilize the food you are given it has a negative effect on you. Similarly, if you ingest too much spiritual food and don't allow it to change you then you can become complacent.

3. Your respiratory system: the Hebrew word for spirit is *ruach* and it means "air in motion" or "breath". When we breathe in and out we are reminded of how dependent we are on God's Spirit. Are you dependent on His Spirit?

4. Your heart: are you still in love with God and want to spend time with Him? Do you love God with all your body, soul, and mind and your neighbour as yourself? Is your life in tune with God's beating heart?

5. Your gastrointestinal tract: are you digesting the right food? Are you eating a balanced diet of reading the Old and New Testaments?

6. Your eyes: are you focused on the right things? Do you have vision and direction for your life?

7. Your hearing: are you hearing the word of God?

8. Your reflexes: do you react to people and situations as God wants us to?

9. Your hands: do you use your hands for God's purposes? In what way do you serve Him? What is your financial giving like?

10. Your feet: are they walking in the right direction? Do you go to the right places?

These are just some questions we can ask ourselves. They may prompt us to consider areas we may need to focus on. Like a physical health check, they can enable us to ensure we are growing as we should. We all want to be well, to be able to make healthier choices, regardless of our circumstances, and to minimize the risk and impact of existing problems. All this can be achieved by having an annual spiritual health check.

PRAYER

Thank You Father that You hear us when we pray.

Thank You that You can show us Your word. You give us vision and direction for our life.

Thank You that we are guided by You about what we do with our hands, our feet, our lives.

Into Your hands we give our lives.

Direct us and help us to be in tune with You and Your Spirit.

In Jesus' name,

Amen.

CHAPTER 10

When Belief Catches Our Notice

One of my favourite Bible passages is in the New Testament: Hebrews 11:4 to the end of the chapter. Rather than being a "Hall of Fame", it really is a "Hall of Faith", recounting the stories of some of the great heroes of faith. It encourages me every time I read it as I hear about how other people, those who believe in Jesus, have struggled but have kept going. It's like plunging into a pool of cold water on a hot day, refreshing the tired and weary soul.

In this chapter I'd like us to look at personal faith. We know that faith in God means so much more than believing that He created the universe. For believers, our faith is a way of life. In Hebrews 11, Paul gives us a brief history lesson, highlighting the lives of these faith heroes we may have heard about through Sunday school or in school assemblies. From Abel, Enoch, and Noah to Abraham, Sarah, Moses, and David, they lived lives that were characterized by a dependency on God and a desire to grow in a relationship with Him.

In verse 4 we are introduced to Abel and the verse ends with the words: "but through his faith he still speaks" (NRSV). *The Message* puts it this way:

> By an act of faith, Abel brought a better sacrifice to God than Cain. It was what he believed, not what he brought, that made the difference. That's what God noticed and approved as righteous. After all these centuries, that belief continues to catch our notice.

The phrase I want to highlight here is "that belief continues to catch our notice". Belief like that still catches our notice and impacts our own faith today.

We all have stories to share about our lives – about how our faith has made a difference. We also feel encouraged when we hear other people's stories and sometimes we realize that they have had a tougher time than us. Far from delighting in the fact that there are people in worse situations than our own, we are in fact building ourselves up. One way we can increase our own faith's ability to stretch when we are in difficult circumstances is to read or listen to the stories of others. When we share our testimony we encourage others to believe in God and His promises. And when we hear others' testimonies the same thing happens to us.

My story

I first became a Christian when I was fourteen. For most of my early childhood I travelled the world with my parents and siblings as my dad was in the army. I remember Dad reading us Bible stories, our going to Sunday school in Germany, and having a Christian headmaster in Malaysia, but I don't really recollect any serious connection to church life. I do, however, remember praying earnestly every night to our creator God for a sister. That prayer was answered when I was five! Then in the 1980s Dad left the army and we settled in the north of Scotland in the county of Caithness. We could look out of Mum and Dad's bedroom window and see the Pentland Firth between the mainland and Orkney.

Dad worked long hours at an American Naval communication base, often leaving in the early morning and not returning until late at night. Family time was often everyone joining in with the chores as my parents were renovating and extending an old barn.

I quickly settled into this new life and met a friend at school who invited me to the Christian Union. Her name was Valerie. She persuaded me to go on a Christian holiday with Scripture Union.[1] Mum agreed and I helped sell household products door to door to raise the funds to go. On the first night of the holiday, on 7 July 1984, I heard about how God was interested in me. I remember seeing a cartoon-like film of the crucifixion and what stood out for me was the fact that Jesus forgave Peter despite the fact that Peter denied Him. I remember thinking that Jesus asked Peter to feed his sheep three times, the exact number of times Peter denied him. I realized that Jesus died so we could be forgiven. That evening I also started reading Joni Eareckson Tada's book *Joni*[2] and I could not put it down. Joni's story really impacted me as someone who learned to trust God despite what happened in her life.

Keen to grow in this newfound faith I tried to encourage my parents to attend our local church which was in the neighbouring village. Occasionally they would take me or I got a lift with a kindly neighbour. I found it tough as I did not know many people of my age or many who believed the same as me. It was a traditional Free Church of Scotland congregation[3] where they stood to pray, sat to sing, and used the modern psalter as their song book. There was no music except the beautiful voices singing the psalms, and women were not allowed to pray in public. I loved the fact that there was a strong emphasis on the word of God and the grounding I received there has made such a difference to my life. I am thankful to God for the background in Scripture I was given by wonderful Sunday school teachers such as Mary Swanson. Although I struggled to understand why some churches were different from the one I attended, later on I became a fully fledged member of the fellowship.

When I was fifteen and attending one of the Free Church of Scotland camps I realized that I knew God and Jesus but had not realized that God had sent His Spirit to help us. I was reading through the book of Acts at the time and asked God to make me more dependent on His Spirit. I suddenly started speaking in a different language I had not learned – this is what the Bible calls the gift of tongues. I realized I wanted to learn more about this and about different expressions of church. So I started writing to the authors of Christian books I came across, people like Tony Ralls, Brother Andrew, and David Wilkerson. They wrote back and sent me other books to read. My life was really impacted by their stories: I regularly received letters of encouragement and I also knew that they were praying for my family. Years later I was able to meet some of these wonderful people and thank them for encouraging me in my Christian faith and praying for my family.

* * *

You know the feeling when you turn up at an event and someone is wearing the same outfit as you? A couple of years ago I turned up in church to discover one of the older members of our congregation – Jackie – had the same deep purple corduroy coat as me. It was actually quite encouraging because she is an amazing lady and I wanted – and still want – to be like her. Her belief continues to catch our notice.

Jackie

Jackie Jackson was born on the 25 June 1932 in Liverpool. Her early childhood was idyllic until the outbreak of the Second World War when she was evacuated during the blitz of Liverpool docks. It was during this time that Jackie had rheumatic fever and ended up in the local hospital. Unbeknown to Jackie, her precious mother and father died while she was in hospital and she ended up living with Auntie Lal, a family friend, after some time with a very strict foster family.

Aunty Lal insisted that Jackie and her brother attend church. Jackie committed her life to Jesus while attending church but it was not until later, during her nursing training, that she finally nailed her colours to the cross determined to live for Jesus. She attended an Easter service all dolled up in a green suit and Easter bonnet!

She went on to train as a midwife and then back to Walton Hospital in Liverpool where she had been during her training in neurology. A lot of Jackie's friends were talking about going on to work as missionaries. At one meeting at Keswick Bible Week Jackie stood up and committed to do the same – even though she didn't really mean it! At this point she was undecided about what God wanted her to do. Her head was turned again when she went to a hospital dance and a prominent neurosurgeon told Jackie she would get a sought-after new nursing post if she applied. God, however, had other plans and she felt she couldn't apply for the post as she was reminded of her original call to the mission field.

Jackie then studied for three years at Emmanuel Bible College in Birkenhead. During this time she was frustrated as she was unsure about where God wanted her. She was interested in Bible translation but did not think she was clever enough to do it – she thought she had to be a Cambridge or Oxford graduate.

After she graduated she went in to nursing for a while before she realized she could apply to Wycliffe Bible Translators. Wycliffe accepted Jackie and she had some further training with them.

Jackie was determined to go where the gospel had not been heard before, and, on 19 November 1962, she undertook a 24-hour journey through Mexico to a little airfield in the middle of nowhere. After six weeks of initial training, which included learning survival skills, she headed to an Indian tribe in South America.

Jackie spent thirty-odd years with her new family. Her midwifery and nursing skills proved invaluable on many an occasion. Just before she was due to take retirement Jackie started having problems with her eyesight. When her symptoms got worse and she realized her mouth, throat, and lungs were also affected Jackie headed back to the UK. She was diagnosed with dystonia, a neurological disorder where there are sustained muscle contractions and repetitive movements. Usually present from birth it can develop after severe illness or trauma.

She was heart-broken when she had to tell her friends back in South America about her diagnosis and the fact there was no treatment. "Come back to us," was their reply "you might as well be with us in that case." So Jackie headed back to the jungle until 16 May 1996, when increasing poor health forced her to return home.

Since then Jackie has been an active member of our church family. Every day she struggles with her disease and the challenges it brings. Looking at this wee lady you would not realize she is really an Exocet missile wrapped in the fabric of a purple coat.

About Ken

My Dad, Ken, is approaching his seventies and has fought many battles. He was born 20 July 1946 to Poppy and Gordon Hunter in County Durham. This was post-war Britain during which time there was rationing and poverty. Dad made the choice in his teenage years that he would join the army as a boy soldier, even though he did well at school and could have gone to university, as he knew his wage would help his family's finances. He trained first as a mechanical and electrical engineer, and later with radar.

A brave man and a hard worker, he fought in the Oman crisis in the mid-1970s and saw sights he would rather forget. He had several overseas postings to Germany and Malaysia and left the army as a Warrant Officer, having worked his way up through the ranks. He was well respected by those who worked with him because he had a reputation for getting the job done. He also knew how to have fun – representing the army as an amateur boxer and later as a team player in rugby. He once had concussion for at least a week after playing rugby and no one really knew until he recovered!

Mum and Dad met at their local church where I think their minister did a bit of matchmaking. My twin brother Paul and I were christened in the same church by a tearful vicar who had helped with the matchmaking! Dad was a man who was willing to help anyone – even while Mum was in labour he was fixing the gas and air supply and various other bits of equipment in the maternity unit. Five years after my twin brother and I were born, while we were based in Germany, my sister Lorna came along to complete the family.

It was about this time that Mum and Dad bought an old ruin of a house in the north of Scotland, having been given a property newspaper by a lady in The Salvation Army. Years later I remember Dad telling me that he was sure that God had been guiding them. While overseas they had the house renovated and the whole family moved to Scotland in the 1980s. Dad started work at the American communication base in Caithness. Such was his strong work ethic that he would leave for work early each morning, arriving home after dark; all his spare time was spent completing the house or helping his neighbours.

In 1985 Dad came to know in a more personal way the God he was interested in. It was such an exciting time because over a three-year period I saw the whole family come to a personal understanding of God.

Dad later told me he remembers God challenging him to serve Him before he met my mum but he didn't obey that original call. He strongly felt that he had been given a second chance: he could see God's fingerprints in his life and he learned to trust God for himself and his family. Later Dad felt called to train as a minister and, after an arduous few years of preparation and a period of time separated from the family, he did just that. Prior to his ordination and permanent posting both Mum and Dad worked in a large care home where Mum was a carer and Dad was a handy man – perhaps preparing them both for the future.

Dad's later working life was as a minister working in a small village called Brora in Sutherland, Scotland, and as a hospital chaplain. After nearly a decade in full-time church ministry he took early retirement to care for Mum who was in renal failure. When Mum went into remission they moved to Nottingham to be nearer to my sister, Lorna, and her family.

Just before the move to Nottingham Mum began to realize that Dad had some memory issues and sensed that this would probably be his final battle. He was finally diagnosed with early-onset Alzheimer's disease three years ago. The cause is unknown but it has been suggested that it may be due to the chemicals Dad was exposed to in his army life. The only in-depth conversation I have had with Dad about his illness was when he told me that he knew he had memory issues but he knew he could trust God. He now struggles to have any conversation about it. Dad may once have been able to wire a whole house but now he can't even wire a plug. He is a man of faith who knows where he is heading – his belief catches our notice.

There are times when I have been to see Dad and I know he is struggling to know who I am. A few weeks ago I returned home on the train and felt overcome with emotion. I felt like it was swirling round me – a dark oppressive cloud like the dementors in the Harry Potter books. I realized what it was – it was the dark stain of grief and death pressing into my life again. I could feel this feeling whirling inside and knew if I cried all the past feelings of loss would bubble to the surface. Crying to God He allowed me to remember He was still with me, that Dad was still present, and in that His grace and mercy He was allowing me to walk through grief slowly this time.

I went to see Mum and Dad at the start of July this summer. We had just lost Jim Graham, one of our previous pastors at Gold Hill Baptist Church. While with my parents I typed into the internet Dad's old army regiment and his name. There was a message on a forces website asking if anyone knew my dad. I think it had been there for a number of years. The person asking had found a diary that her dad and my dad had written together while on duty in Malaysia. No one knew it even existed. I wrote wondering how long the request had been there and if they would get my reply.

The following Sunday morning, having been to our home church, mourning Jim's loss, I received a message from the website enquirer. They had the diary and were sending me a copy. God stepped in and reminded me that although I was losing Dad, God knew his whole story and was giving me something I never knew existed about him.

In John 6:68 Peter says to the Lord, "To whom can we go? You have the words of eternal life"(NRSV). When life is confusing, complicated, and challenging, these people – those whose faith catches our notice – remind us that we can trust in the one who is at the centre of it all.

Hebrews 11:32–40 (NLT) says,

> *How much more do I need to say? It would take too long to recount the stories of the faith of Gideon, Barak, Samson, Jephthah, David, Samuel, and all the prophets. By faith these people overthrew kingdoms, ruled with justice, and received what God had promised them. They shut the mouths of lions, quenched the flames of fire, and escaped death by the edge of the sword. Their weakness was turned to strength. They became strong in battle and put whole armies to flight. Women received their loved ones back again from death. But others were tortured, refusing to turn from God in order to be set free. They placed their hope in a better life after the resurrection.*

PRAYER

Father,

Thank You for reminding us of other heroes of our faith that encourage us to keep going no matter how hard the terrain.

Thank You for reminding us that many others have gone before us.

Thank You that You have something better in mind for us. Thank You that You give us a reason and a hope.

In Jesus' name,

Amen.

CHAPTER 11

Keep a Vibrant Heart

Guard your heart

I was seventeen years old and desperate to experience life outside the community I had been a part of for the past seven years. I was so excited as I was leaving home, moving from the north of Scotland to Dundee – a day's journey south of Caithness – to study for a degree in nursing at Dundee College of Technology. I remember saying goodbye to some family friends when one of them said to me: "Guard your heart." I was surprised and wondered why he had said what he had. He was quoting Proverbs 4:23–27 to a young woman keen to explore the world. What he was telling me to do was guard my heart, keep strong in the faith, and keep focused.

> *Keep vigilant, watch over your heart;*
> *that's where life starts.*
>
> *Don't talk out of both sides of your mouth;*
> *avoid careless banter, white lies, and gossip.*
>
> *Keep your eyes straight ahead;*
> *ignore all sideshow distractions.*

Watch your step,
and the road will stretch out smooth before you.

Look neither right nor left;
leave evil in the dust.

Proverbs 4:23–27, *The Message*

Years later, and I am sitting waiting for my youngsters to return from a night out. It is getting later and later – it's nearly midnight. I am sitting in front of the TV wondering what time they will be home. They eventually turn up, noisy enough to wake the sleeping dogs, even though they thought they were being quiet. I had been dozing on and off since eleven waiting for them. It felt as if they had been out for ages; in reality three of our teenagers had simply been spending time in the 24/7 prayer room in our village.

Noisy, jesting, laughing, and sharing what they felt God was telling them, the room quickly filled with colour and joy reflecting their vibrant hearts. So often we are reminded to guard our hearts, but here I want to focus on what keeps our heart vibrant.

What does the heart do?

When the Bible talks about the heart it is not necessarily talking about this physiological organ that pumps blood around the body and to the lungs. In the Bible the word "heart" denotes what is at the centre of a person, reflecting where the heart is actually placed. It is the core or centre of someone, encapsulating feeling and personhood. According to Proverbs 23:7, "For as he thinks in his heart, so *is* he" (NKJV).

The heart is also considered to be the centre of man's

understanding. The Bible is clear about it – our thinking comes from the heart (Genesis 6:5, Daniel 2:30). The Greek philosopher Aristotle in the fourth century BC identified the heart as the centre of vitality in the body – the centre of intelligence and emotion. It was not until the Renaissance period in the sixteenth century that physicians realized that the heart had chambers pumping both oxygenated and deoxygenated blood. It came to be considered as the centre of all things to do with blood and pneuma.

Today we consider the heart to be the centre of our emotions and sometimes it governs our thinking. People enter relationships and end them by following the dictates of their hearts. They buy things because they "set their heart on it". They believe their emotions are what defines them and that it is wrong to repress these feelings.

The Bible teaches us that neither our emotions nor our intellect are as important as knowing what is in the human heart. The heart is used as a metaphor for what is at the centre of our lives. It is about what governs us, what directs us, what our basic objectives are. The great battle we can go through as people is deciding what is our heart's greatest love? What do we love most? What is at the centre of our heart? As 1 Samuel 16:7 states: "The Lord does not look at the things people look at. People look at the outward appearance, but the Lord looks at the heart."

Keeping a healthy heart

According to the WHO, heart disease is the leading cause of death in the UK, USA, Canada, and Australia and yet it is often preventable. Heart disease can occur if there is a build-up of plaque in the walls of the arteries as a result of high cholesterol (from fatty diets) in the bloodstream, or cigarette smoke. The arteries can become furred up in the same way pipes in a plumbing system can be affected by limescale. This furring makes it harder for blood to flow through.

As Christians we can allow spiritual plaque to build up with the resultant development of "heart disease". Our character and behaviour can lead to temporary blockages such as unforgiveness or persistent damaging habits. Just as people may have silent cardiovascular disease for many years before it explodes into their lives with devastating effects, so too the impact of spiritual "heart disease" can be just as unexpected, bringing the sudden realization that we have turned from God.

Maybe we have been digesting the wrong spiritual food or perhaps we have not been practising the spiritual disciplines as we should. The best remedy is to take preventive measures to ensure that this does not become a problem for us in the future. It is always helpful to look at ways to increase our resilience, perhaps implementing small spiritual lifestyle changes to bolster it. Let's determine before God to be pro-active and not complacent.

How can we avoid complacency?

The heart is a muscle and like any muscle it needs to be exercised. We need to keep turning to the Cross and be reminded of God's outrageous love for us. Sometimes we don't do that and we can become complacent. I tend to think of spiritual complacency as the equivalent of physical heart disease.

We all know people who we might label as complacent because we have probably all experienced this at some point in our Christian lives. The best way to describe complacency is to define it in terms of its opposite; its opposite being zeal. The kind of zeal I am talking about is not the fanatical religious zeal associated with suicide bombers that we read about in the media at the moment. The zeal I am talking about is motivated by our desire to love God.

John Rainolds (Reynolds), born in 1549, was an English academic and Puritan who was a delegate at the Hampton Court Conference where he was involved in the translation of the King James Bible. He defined Christian zeal as "an earnest desire and concern for all things pertaining to the glory of God and the kingdom of the Lord Jesus among men".[1] It is this zeal that causes our hearts to pump, and our minds to focus on the pursuit of God: this is what delights God.

Complacency, on the other hand, is when we are satisfied with life and are unaware of oncoming danger. Kodak is a recognizable label – it was once an internationally successful and well-known household name. But in 2012 Kodak went bankrupt. Very few people expected it, just like the retailer British Home Stores' failure in the summer of 2016. Kodak went bankrupt not because of financial mismanagement, but because of complacency. They did not see the danger coming – they did not predict the mass impact of the digital age nor the threat to their business.

So, we need to be at peace with where we are but dedicated to see change, passionate to push forward.

Practical ways we can keep a vibrant heart

What helps to keep our hearts beating in rhythm with God's? I have listed below a small selection from among the many approaches we can take. The most important thing we can do is to allow God to be in control of our hearts. He should be at the centre of our lives. There is no "I" in heart but there is a "He".

Remember the blessings

Sometimes when life is busy we forget to remember our blessings. When life was not as busy as it is now I would sit once a week and write out the blessings I had experienced each week. Perhaps the best time to do this is when we are struggling with the pressures of life so we are reminded that there *is* good working in our lives.

Strengthen your prayer life

We have already talked about some of the spiritual disciplines we can use. There are also some practical steps we can take to do this, such as joining a prayer triplet or attending a regular prayer group. I have a WhatsApp group set up with two friends and we try and meet together once a month. Not only has God really blessed us through that group, but I am also aware that it has really strengthened my prayer life – it has been extremely motivational for me. Thank you Jane and Helen.

Be an encourager

Let's intentionally set out to listen to people who need to be encouraged. One little random act of kindness a day can transform someone's day, week, or month. I think it is often in the act of encouraging others that we ourselves are also encouraged.

Create a sense of gratefulness rather than negativity

Negative attitudes and thoughts can make us feel helpless and hopeless. This in turn can upset the body's delicate balance of hormones and reduce the chemicals needed by the brain to help us feel happy and content. It can even have a negative impact on the terminal ends of our DNA strands which help us age well. These are the physical and psychological impacts of a negative spirit.

Being grateful is one of the essentials in life. We are not necessarily born grateful, but we can and should respond to our Creator God with a thankful heart.

Brené Brown is an American scholar and research professor at the University of Houston Graduate College of Social Work. She is also a friend of Oprah Winfrey. In her study of vulnerability Brené Brown tells us: "It's not joy that makes us grateful; it is gratitude that makes us joyful."[2] Interestingly, speaking of vulnerability, she helpfully points out: "[vulnerability] is the core of shame and fear and our struggle for worthiness but it appears that it is also the birthplace of joy, of creativity, of belonging, of love."[3] As Christians, our place of vulnerability should be at the Cross, which is also the birthplace of joy, creativity, belonging, and love.

Be quick to forgive

The Australian Institute of Family Counselling (AIFC) suggests that forgiveness is the "key that unlocks your heart in order to bring about healing and change."[4] We know that unforgiveness can lead to heartache. Think of all the families that feud for years because they have not been able to practise forgiveness. Jesus was quite clear when He said: "For if you forgive others their trespasses, your heavenly Father will also forgive you, but if you do not forgive others their trespasses, neither will your Father forgive your trespasses" (Matthew 6:14–15, ESV). And Paul urges us with these words: "Let all bitterness and wrath and anger and clamour and slander be put away from you, along with all malice. Be kind to one another, tenderhearted, forgiving one another, as God in Christ forgave you" (Ephesians 4:31–32, ESV).

Turn your anxiety and worry over to God

We know the effect of raised anxiety levels on the heart (see Chapter 6). Dr Una McCann is a professor of psychiatry and behavioural sciences at the world-renowned Johns Hopkins Hospital in Baltimore, Maryland. She believes that anxiety disorders play a major part in heart disease. Certainly we know that generalized anxiety disorders are linked with a higher incidence of cardiovascular events such as strokes, heart attacks, heart failure, and even death.

The above strategies are not new suggestions and they can be summarized in what the sixteenth- and seventeenth-century English reformers – the Puritans – considered to be the four means through which God can stir up Christians to ensure they keep a vibrant heart.

1. *Prayer.* We can ask God to rekindle the flame in our heart to love and serve Him. I would suggest that prayer can be in any form. Jesus prayed in a variety of ways and places.

2. *God's word.* Individual study and listening to the preaching of God's word is invaluable. You may struggle to take time to do this in the world we live in. Think strategy, problem solving – why not have the Bible on CD in your car? Have soundbites of Scripture and its teaching in your home, posted on calendars, or in daily devotional books. Like a snack it will help you when you are busy – but remember you do need to have a full meal on a regular basis!

3. *Fellowship.* In simple terms this is our church attendance – we should be clear that failing to meet together is something to be avoided (Hebrews 10:25). We need to spend time with other people who believe the same as us: house groups, small groups, church meetings – places we can meet other Christians.

4. *Repentance.* Repenting for sins committed and growing in the desire and ability to resist future sin. This will stop our heart growing cold.

Malcolm and I were recently at a large event in the south of Ireland where he was invited to preach at a celebratory event in the Church of Ireland. There were some visiting dignitaries from America – including two bishops. After Malcolm had preached they came and thanked him for the message. One of them told Malcolm how it had really helped him but that things were so different in his own church. Malcolm was confused and asked him to explain, to which the bishop replied: "In our church we don't have someone speaking for that length of time." What he meant was that they have an order of service they use but no one actually preaches. Malcolm suggested that they consider changing it, reminding them that people can be encouraged through listening to the word of God and preaching.

We allow ourselves to become dried out or burned out if we don't meet with other Christians or listen to God's word. In the seventeenth century William Fenner wrote:

> *The coals that lie together in the hearth, you*
> *see how they glow and are fired, while the little*
> *coals that are fallen off, and lie by, separate from*
> *their company, are black without fire. If ever*
> *thou desirest to be zealous, make much of the*
> *fellowship of the saints.*[5]

The coals that glow hottest are the coals that lie closest together.

Hara Estroff Marano, editor of *Psychology Today*, has written:

> *At the heart of resilience is a belief in oneself—yet*
> *also a belief in something larger than oneself.*
> *Resilient people do not let adversity define them.*
> *They find resilience by moving towards a goal*
> *beyond themselves, transcending pain and grief*
> *by perceiving bad times as a temporary state of*
> *affairs... It's possible to strengthen your inner self*

and your belief in yourself, to define yourself as capable and competent. It's possible to fortify your psyche. It's possible to develop a sense of mastery.[6]

At the heart of resilience for the Christian is the belief in something larger than ourselves – God. He is our Creator. He reaches into our broken world and offers a pathway back to Him through the life of His son. Let's allow Him to be at the centre of our heart. He has done so much for us **and** He has given us everything we need for daily living. Trust Him – let Him guide you.

PRAYER

Father, our prayer is a simple one: please be at the centre of our hearts.

In Jesus' name,

Amen.

CHAPTER 12

Walking with a Limp

Derek Redmond was born in 1965. He is now a retired British athlete and during his career he held the British record for the 400m sprint, and won gold medals in the 4x400m relay at the World Championships, European Championships, and Commonwealth Games. His most important race, the one he is best remembered for, is not one he won but one he lost during the 1992 Olympics in Barcelona.

Redmond's career had been blighted by a series of injuries that consistently interrupted his performance. At the 1988 Olympics in Seoul he had to pull out of the opening round of the 400m just ninety seconds before his heat because of an Achilles tendon injury. By the time of the 1992 Olympics he had undergone eight operations due to injuries, and then, during the 400m semi-final, he tore his hamstring about 175 metres from the finish line. The hamstring is a group of four muscles that run along the back of the thigh. They allow us to bend our legs at the knee, to put one foot in front of the other, and even to run. Derek tried to continue and fell to the ground in pain. He struggled to his feet in an attempt to continue the race and then, in an unforgettably graphic image of love and support, his father Jim Redmond barged through security and joined Derek on the track. His father helped him get up and together they managed to complete the full lap of the track, crossing the finish line as the 65,000-crowd gave a standing ovation.[1] Derek called it the day that changed his life and it is recorded as one of the top three memorable moments in Olympic history.

On 10 January 2012, Derek's father, Jim, was one of the Olympic torch bearers in London in the lead-up to that summer's Olympic Games. Derek is now a motivational speaker sharing his story to inspire people as they run the race. People still stop him in the street to ask him about that day in 1992.

In Genesis 32:22–24, Jacob was about to cross the River Jabbok, which means "crooked river". Up until that time Jacob's life had been one of lies and deceit. His very name Jacob means "deceiver" or "grabber", a note that harmonizes well with the idea of the crooked river, Jabbok.

Jacob had cheated his brother Esau out of his birthright and the day of reckoning was fast approaching: he was about to meet Esau with the 400 men who had threatened to kill Jacob. That night Jacob was at a place called Peniel (in Hebrew this word means "the face of God"). While there he was attacked and wrestled with a "man" until daybreak. Jacob did not know who he was wrestling against; if he had known from the outset that his opponent was God, perhaps he would not have engaged with him. As they wrestled, Jacob was face to face with God.

The strangest thing in the story is that Jacob was not defeated until the man "touched the socket of his thigh; so the socket of Jacob's thigh was dislocated while he wrestled with him" (verse 25, NASB). Despite this, Jacob would not let go of the man. He pleaded: "I will not let you go unless you bless me" (verse 26, NASB). These were the words of someone who was subdued, beaten, crippled even, and yet begging for a blessing. The event was so significant that Jacob's life was radically changed (verse 28). Even his name was changed, from Jacob to Israel, and he still walked with a limp, crooked like the stream where he came to face to face with God. Jacob's self-reliant behaviour was broken as he learned to lean on God. All his life Jacob had used people for his own ends, but from that point onward God showed Jacob that he needed to rely on Him. In the same way, when we lean on God He blesses us.

What do Derek Redmond and Jacob have in common? The obvious thing is that they were both injured and yet they persevered – they still continued the race. Sometimes we have to persevere while carrying injuries or the scars of past events that remind us of where we have come from. We have to walk with a limp. Life is hard – stuff happens along its journey but we know the end and we can turn our eyes to Heaven. We also have people, like Derek's father Jim, who help us on the way.

So what helps us to persevere? What enables us to keep going? In the following sections I want to concentrate on three ideas as we seek to answer these questions.

Training in the trials

Before we do anything we usually count the cost of what is involved, from going out for a meal to agreeing to run a marathon. Malcolm and I are currently renovating a small bungalow by the sea in Ireland. It took us a year to decide what to do with it. Before we contracted the builder we had to go through planning, have building regulations sorted, and look at costings. Jesus used a similar illustration, asking who would not count the cost before building a tower (Luke 14:25–34).

We know that being a Christian does not mean that life is suddenly easier. It is not a prescription for a smooth, uncomplicated life. Jesus advises us to count the cost before we choose to follow Him, and to know that it won't be easy.

As I write, the 2016 Olympics are being held in Rio de Janeiro in Brazil. One of the amazing stories from this Games is the inclusion of a refugee team. Yusra Mardini is an eighteen-year-old Syrian refugee who is participating as a swimmer. Her story of courage during training encourages the soul. Before finding sanctuary in Germany, Yusra and her sister Sarah joined eighteen other refugees fleeing to Europe from Turkey in a dinghy. As they crossed the Aegean Sea, the overloaded boat began to sink. Yusra and Sarah dived into the water and, between them, pushed the boat for three-and-a-half hours until they reached safety, landing on the Greek island of Lesbos. At the Games, Yusra made it through to the 100m butterfly swimming heats before eventually being beaten. Her story is one of trial and training.

We all find it hard to understand why our good and loving Father allows bad things to happen. Why do we have to experience trials and tribulations? It may be old-fashioned to say that one of the purposes for the trials that we go through is to perfect perseverance in us: the ability to cling to God in every circumstance without letting go. God allows us to go through trials and they are part of the mystery of working all things together for good. Ultimately, He wants us to grow more like His Son and to be dependent on His strength.

In 2 Corinthians 12:9–10 Paul talks about his struggles with something he refers to in verse 7 as the "thorn in his flesh", the inference for us being that it caused him pain and was a significant trial. Each time Paul prayed to have this taken away, God reminded him: "My grace is all you need. My power works best in weakness" (ESV).

We are also learning to train in the trials. James picks up this theme in his letter (James 1:1–11), reminding us that God wants us to trust Him in the trials of life. We can trust Him in the middle of them as He uses trials to mould and change us so we can become more like Jesus. *The Message* version of James 1:2–4 puts it this way:

> Consider it a sheer gift, friends, when tests and challenges come at you from all sides. You know that under pressure, your faith-life is forced into the open and shows its true colours. So don't try to get out of anything prematurely. Let it do its work so you become mature and well-developed, not deficient in any way.

And 1 Peter 1:6–7 exhorts us:

> In all this you greatly rejoice, though now for a little while you may have had to suffer grief in all kinds of trials. These have come so that the proven genuineness of your faith – of greater worth than gold, which perishes even though refined by fire – may result in praise, glory and honour when Jesus Christ is revealed.

This is "because we know that suffering produces perseverance; perseverance, character, and character hope. And hope does not put us to shame, because God's love has been poured out into our hearts through the Holy Spirit" (Romans 5:3–5).

Sometimes we just don't know why we have to go through particular trials. In the words of Isaiah 55:8–9: "For my thoughts are not your thoughts, neither are your ways my ways... As the heavens are higher than the earth, so are my ways higher than your ways and my thoughts than your thoughts."

We simply need to know that God is there and one day we will reach the end of the race.

Keeping an eye on the end of the race

A few years ago someone organized some wonderful days away for us in the Lake District – one of our favourite places to go. However, there was a small problem – I had a tear in my Achilles tendon (although at the time I did not realize it was so serious). It had been quite painful for a few weeks and I didn't want to miss out on our trip. I packed my walking boots, determined that my sore foot would not stop me. We managed to go on a few long walks, with my foot strapped into my walking boots.

It was not until I got home that I realized I had to see someone about it. I was stretching up to put something on the top of my wardrobe one morning after our trip away when I felt the tendon tear. I later found out that it was a rare side-effect of the antibiotics I had been taking for a chest infection. They had caused tendonitis, particularly affecting my Achilles tendon. A trip to the emergency room revealed the truth and I ended up on crutches and had to wear a supportive boot for a while. It was a horrible time but I had not wanted to miss the time we had away or the chance to see the beautiful countryside in the Lake District. I had endured the pain because I wanted to keep going. There was a reward at the end!

The athlete Derek Redmond wanted to finish his race so much that he struggled to get off the ground and keep walking the last 175 metres. He had developed perseverance because he had experienced the ups and downs of training. Perseverance can be defined as "persistence in doing something despite difficulty or delay in achieving success".[2] Derek was able to persevere despite the terrible pain. It didn't matter that the Olympic Committee disqualified him – he finished the race!

Athletes describe mental toughness or grit as their ability to consistently perform toward the upper range of their talent and skill regardless of any competitive circumstances. They keep going even though their brain is saying, "Stop, you can't keep going." One way they can do this is by using the skill of visualization or guided imagery when they mentally train themselves to push through any barriers they face. They create a mental image or intention of what they want to happen or feel in reality. Using this technique they can focus on the intended outcome, standing in the moment by imagining the scene, complete with images of a previous best performance, how it felt, or even sounded (the roar of the crowd). In the words of Allyson Felix, the three-time world 200m champion: "I find visualisation really works for me – thinking through in slow motion everything I'm going to do."[3]

The most effective form of visualization occurs when the technique is repeated several times. Athletes performing it feel they have a sense of control over the race and a strong belief in their own ability. Allyson Felix regularly uses this technique to prepare for her races.

I am not suggesting that we use this technique to run races. I do think we need to remind ourselves where we are headed and that Jesus is with us as we run the race. In enduring what life throws at us let's remember that He is with us.

Samantha Gash is an endurance athlete who converted to ultra marathons after completing her first marathon. In 2010, at the age of twenty-five, she took a semester off from law school to race 155 miles through the Chilean desert in the Atacama Crossing. In 2012 she ran non-stop for 379 km (235 miles) across the Simpson Desert in Australia. She has also run the 250-mile race through the Gobi Desert, which she describes as the most mentally gruelling of all the races she has completed. She uses the technique of visualization when she is in immense pain and feels she can't continue. She tries to focus her mind on the positive of completing. In the documentary *Desert Runners* she speaks of her body and mind being stronger than she could ever imagine.[4]

I don't think I will ever be like Samantha, but I recently took part in a 5 km race for a cancer charity. I may never be the first woman and youngest person to complete the Four Desert Grand Slam but before I did the 5 km I didn't think I would ever be able to run even 1 km! I really wanted to run or walk the race that day remembering a wonderful woman called Louise and raise money to help fight breast cancer. In fact, this book is dedicated to the amazing Knight family and the memory of Louise.

Our body and mind are stronger than we think. As Christians, we can challenge and train ourselves to compete in the most demanding of races. We may not want to use the visualization technique but we can keep focused. When the terrain is rough and unfriendly we can strengthen ourselves with the unshakable knowledge that one day we will complete this race. We are on the winning side.

For endurance athletes, persistence or perseverance is particularly crucial as it helps them to stick to a difficult and gruelling training schedule. They know that nothing can make them compromise their regime, no matter how tired they may feel. It's not just about preparing the muscles and getting fit, the regime reminds them of why they are doing it and who they are. Ultimately it gives them the confidence they need when the starting gun fires and the race begins.

As Christians we can use these techniques to help us keep going even though we are tired, in pain, and wanting to stop. Using all the techniques covered in this book, a spiritual fitness regime to improve our resilience will give us the confidence we need as we run the race. We also know where we are heading, just like Paul when he wrote: "I press on toward the goal for the prize of the heavenly call of God in Christ Jesus" (Philippians 3:14; NRSV).

We are not on our own

Derek Redmond had true perseverance but also he didn't have to run the race by himself. His father was there at the very moment when he needed him to help him get up and complete the final metres. Our Heavenly Father is watching us and is able to intervene when we need Him to. Sometimes He has to put His arms around us and remind us that He is with us – and that's OK as we just want to finish the race.

Jenny Susser is a clinical health psychologist. Specializing in sports psychology, she formerly worked at the Women's Sports Medicine Center at the Hospital for Special Surgery in New York City. She suggests that athletes who perform endurance sports have certain personality traits: persistence, endless curiosity, a lack of fear when it comes to failure, and a sense of boldness.

The amazing fact is that, as Christians, we also have the personality traits needed to compete as an endurance athlete. We can be persistent, bold, and fearless. We sometimes forget that we have God's Spirit living in us – the very same God who spoke the word at creation lives within us.

Our God also knows what is in front of us and can prepare us for the way ahead. Sometimes He changes the path.

The Greek word *diastrepho* (διαστρεφω) means "to turn away (from the right path)" and it also carries the idea of "to make crooked, perverse or misleading". For example, it is found in Acts 13:8 where Elymas the magician turns against God. If we turn *to* God rather than *away* from Him, He will help us. Our God is able to help us by making the path straight: "What a God!" says the psalmist, "His road stretches straight and smooth. Every God-direction is road tested. Everyone who runs toward him makes it." (Psalm 18:30, *The Message*). And addressing King Cyrus, God says: "I will go before thee, and make the crooked places straight" (Isaiah 45:2, KJV).

We know that we may have trials along the road, and we are reminded that the Christian journey is not easy. The Polish poet Stanisław Jerzy Lec once said, "He who limps is still walking".

What should encourage us is that the trials actually help us: we are in training in the trials, maturing in our faith, and growing more like Jesus. We can also keep our eyes on the end of the race. We know the end of the story – what lies ahead. And finally, we are never on our own.

PRAYER

Dear Father,

Thank You that You are with us no matter what we experience.

Thank You for reminding us that You are with us, and that we are not running the race on our own. Thank You that You have given us Your Holy Spirit to strengthen and guide us.

We ask that You would make our crooked paths straight, and grant us a vision of what You want us to do and where we are going.

Help us to lean on You as Jacob did and remind us that one day we will see You face to face.

In Jesus' name,

Amen.

CHAPTER 13

Living Under a Promise

As Christians we are living under a covenant or a relationship with our Father. The word covenant refers to an agreement between two parties. It comes from the Latin word *convenīre*, which means "to come together" or agree. The orginal Hebrew words are *kārat berît*, which means "to cut a covenant" or pact, treaty, or alliance. It is an important concept. The word "covenant" is found 555 times in the Bible, which is nearly as many as the word "faith" (628 times). I suppose the closest thing we have in modern society is the covenants we see in marriage or adoption but they are not quite the same thing. It is a legal contract between parties of equal standing. In the Bible the word covenant is used to describe agreements between people, nations, and God.

In Old Testament times, if a small nation wanted to form an alliance or agreement with a larger nation the leaders would meet and form a covenant. Both leaders would make a promise to pay a tribute of so many talents of gold every year, to be loyal to one another, and the leader of the larger or stronger nation would promise to defend the weaker one. To signify this was an important covenant, they would walk through a pathway of cut-up animals meaning that if they broke their promise then God would treat them like the animals. An example is that of King Zedekiah's covenant with the people of Judah in Jeremiah 34:8–22.

God also made a promise – a covenant to the people of Israel. Throughout the Old Testament the Jewish people operated under the old Mosaic covenant as described in Exodus 19:5. They were reminded again and again that there was a new covenant coming, as in Jeremiah 31:31–34.

When Jesus died and His body was broken God established with us a better covenant: one where the Temple curtain was torn in two. Now access to God could be achieved directly. Luke 22:20 (ESV) says, "And likewise the cup after they had eaten, saying, 'This cup that is poured out for you is the new covenant in my blood.'"

Hebrews 9:15, in the NRSV, says,

> For this reason he is the mediator of a new
> covenant, so that those who are called may
> receive the promised eternal inheritance, because
> a death has occurred that redeems them from the
> transgressions under the first covenant.

As Christians we live under a new covenant of grace. We have a promise that God is with us. His Spirit is at work in us. Sometimes He feels very far away but He is the same, yesterday, today, and forever. What has probably changed is how *we* feel. We may have moved away from God as He does not move away from us. He is not very far away from those who call on His name. Certainly if we are honest with God when we talk to Him – He listens. As Psalm 145:18

says, "The Lord is near to all who call on him, to all who call on him in truth" (NRSV).

We can talk about it – we may know the Scriptures, but some days, weeks, or even months it may feel like He is not near. It really depends on what is going on in our lives. We allow trials and challenges to become our main focus.

In 2000 Duran Duran's song, "The Sun Doesn't Shine Forever" was released on the *Pop Trash* album by Hollywood Records. When I woke up this morning the words of the song were singing in my head. It felt like one of those days when the sun doesn't shine. The weather forecast was for a cloudy day with a 60 per cent chance of rain and no sign of the sun. I was travelling back on the train from Nottingham to London after visiting Mum and Dad. Today my sister and I had to leave Dad at a respite care facility in a local nursing home as Mum is too poorly to care for him. A sad day.

I look at the passing countryside – colours that look sad and dull under the cloudy sky. It's like the countryside knows I am sad. I don't want to be in the dark or shade – I want to see the bright colours of spring and summer bursting into view. Some of the leaves on the trees have not opened yet. The trees stand bare, dark, and eerie against the backdrop of the saddened sky. Guardians of the countryside waiting for the sunlight to filter through their branches and bear growth.

But the sun still shines even though we don't always feel its rays. Even on cloudy days solar panels pick up the electrical energy that is generated from ambient light. Even though I may not feel His presence, the Son still blazes. His light energizes me even when I don't know it and the clouds of life obscure my view.

We don't live under a cloud – we are living under a promise. It's remembering what those promises are and placing them in the forefront of our minds. I often think it's a little like when we are studying for exams. We study, we know the work we need to know. We get up in the morning of the exam to do some last-minute cramming of information and we suddenly feel that we know nothing. The anxiety and fear of the examination has taken hold and we don't remember facts we have learned months before – things that we could have at one time recited backwards while standing on our heads.

I suppose it's about not letting fear and anxiety cloud our view. It's remembering we live under a promise no matter what is going on around us.

Waiting

The struggle I have is living in the gap – the time between an event and waiting for God to change that situation. I think of the times when I had a level of expectancy for Benjamin to be healed, had trusted that family members would come to know Jesus, and that I would have answers to our prayers about practical problems or issues we had in our everyday lives. Faith and trust in His promises are important – in fact essential – but what I have learned is that there is more. I have spent my time waiting for God to act – His hand reaching into my situation and changing it. I have not always appreciated that God's purposes were at work the moment I stepped into "the gap".

I want to tell you about what I call my "rotten summer". It was a time when as a family we were tired and weary because we had a lot of physical and emotional demands on our time and energy. I was travelling to work from Reading to Dulwich, London, every day, which meant that I had a three-hour journey of buses, Tubes, and trains to get there and back. Malcolm was also based in London and was travelling the M25 corridor, clocking in a lot of hours travelling to and fro to external meetings and events. We were fortunate enough to have a lovely house but it was costing us money – it needed so many repairs doing including a whole level of floor joists to be replaced on the first floor right under the family bathroom.

Benjamin had just had another bout of pneumonia and we were struggling with the fact that although he had been infection-free for a few years, we now felt we were taking backward steps. Let's add into the mix the fact I was studying for a Masters and training to be a nurse practitioner – as well as my being on the waiting list for a hysterectomy.

That August we had decided to have a few weeks in our caravan with friends. Malcolm and I were desperate for a break. I think that's what kept me going through the commute in the last few weeks of the summer. On holiday, when driving up quite a steep hill into Exeter, the head gasket blew up in our car. We were towing a caravan and had four children and a dog as passengers. Smoke pumped out of our bonnet and the car came to a standstill. We had to wait for a couple of hours sitting on the roadside as cars tried to get past our broken-down car, caravan, and dream of a relaxing holiday.

Thankfully after our car was picked up, our friend John, a mechanic, managed to negotiate our caravan to be left at a campsite near him. Two weeks later we were home with a £1000-pound bill to fix the car and then the washing machine died. It's not fun when you have two weeks' worth of washing for a family of six. Then even the iron stopped working. (I can sense some of you thinking – that's no loss!)

I think it's fair to say I was feeling sorry for myself. I kept shouting Bible promises to God about how He would look after us. As if He needed to know them! I felt I was standing on the promise of His word but the gap was widening and I feared I might well topple in. At that time I came to realize that when we are in times of trial (even if they are about broken washing machines and head gaskets) it's not about waiting for God to act. God was with me as I loaded washing into the bath and jumped up and down on it with the girls (they still talk about it now!).

But God was with us as we went for a walk and found an orchard full of free apples and pears. On the way home we found a pound coin and bought cream from the corner shop. These were blessings as we were completely broke. We had a feast that night of apple and pear crumble and cream.

God walked with me as I knocked on a neighbour's door and asked to borrow their iron: a whole conversation ensued about life with a neighbour I hardly knew. Absolutely hold onto His promises but remember as you are waiting He is already at work in the gap.

It's not trouble, it's training

I think it's also worth noting that we are all in training. None of us are there yet. We are being changed from one degree of glory into another. We are also partners in this process. God has certainly spent years reminding me and helping me change certain aspects of my character. We have to be intentional about it, allowing God to change how we act and behave.

Brené Brown investigated resilience in her 2015 *New York Times* best-selling book, *Rising Strong*.[1] She interviewed a range of people – from artists to leaders of the Fortune 500 companies – and used a grounded theory approach to ask the question, "What do these people with strong and loving relationships, leaders nurturing creativity, artists pushing innovation, and clergy walking with people through faith and mystery have in common?" Her conclusion was that they recognize the power of emotion and try to make sense of it. She suggests that there are certain people who have emotional intelligence or try to make sense of their behaviour and ask the question, "Why did I respond in that way?"

She gives an example of someone at work in a meeting when a colleague looks at them in a certain way. The immediate response is to punch them or devour a dozen doughnuts. (I think I would like the dozen doughnuts!) She suggests that resilience is available to people who are curious about their behaviour and emotion. Interestingly she also suggests that we live a whole life when we seek a life of authenticity, love, and belonging – and have a resilient spirit. Is that not what the Christian walk is? Being an authentic, loving follower of Jesus who has a strong sense of belonging and identity, and possesses a resilient spirit?

Living a whole life

Living a whole life is not about living for an allocated length of time. Whole life insurance is also known as a "straight life" or "ordinary life" life-insurance policy. It is an insurance policy that remains in place for the entire lifetime of the person who is insured. No, I mean living a whole life being aware of the different components of our lives: body, soul, and mind. It is about being self-aware, knowing that we consist of these three areas and that they interlink in an intimate and intricate way that we may never fully comprehend. It is about knowing the One who made us and that we are fearfully and wonderfully made.

The art of...

The title of this book is *The Art of Daily Resilience*. I consider the process of improving and strengthening our daily resilience as an art. Some may consider it a science and I have mentioned some scientific theory about resilience, but in essence it fits within the field of arts and humanity.

The phrase "the art of" means we can explore the creative fields around resilience. Improving one's resilience is a creative process. Certainly the art of daily resilience is not a passive state. It's not a painting that has been hung on a wall to admire like a Monet or a Manet. It's not a still image of one aspect of our character that we do not need to change or alter. It is an art – something that implies action in a measured way.

Resilience

Throughout this book we have learned about resilience. As I mentioned at the beginning, it is like an elastic band that can be stretched out of shape but which may never go back to the shape it was originally. It is the reeds gently swaying in the afternoon breeze, bending to the wind but returning to their position: bending but not breaking. Let's remind ourselves of Isaiah 42:3: "a bruised reed he will not break". We won't break. God will not break us. He gives us what we need for the circumstances we find ourselves in. He can make us more resilient.

Practical things we can do

There are some practical things we can do to improve our resilience. These are just a few pointers to help you think about exactly what you can do. This is a summary of some of the suggestions peppered throughout this book.

Form an accountability group. This can also be a little like a resiliency support group! Identify a handful of like-minded people who can offer support and encouragement. Meet when you can and keep in touch; use social media for the times when you can't meet. You may want to pray regularly with this group.

Keep a list of Bible verses that inspire you. You don't have to have them all around your house. Recording them in a journal that you can return to when you need to is helpful. Keep them on your phone or sign up online to daily verses to encourage you.

Remind yourself who you are in Jesus. A low self-esteem or wrong view of yourself can impact your resilience. Just like Simba in the Lion King, remember who you are!

Develop a daily self-care routine. This is a little like your daily skincare regime. Identify activities that support you to feel your best and fit it into your daily rhythm of life.

Hopefully this will include activities that help you develop your body, soul, and mind. Think about regular exercise, meditation and prayer, rest, and healthy eating to name just a few. Find out what pattern works for you.

Practise centring yourself in God's presence. Some call this Christian mindfulness. The more we practise being in the moment, holding onto God, then the easier it is to naturally do this when things get tough.

Consider the spiritual disciplines. We have mentioned a few in the chapters of this book. Learn about them and see if they can fit into your daily walk.

PRAYER

Father,

Thank You for reminding us that we are made in Your image – which we consist of in body, soul, and mind. Help us to remain strong in all these areas relying on You and Your strength.

Help us to use the wisdom and creativity You have given us to identify strategies that may help us improve our resilience in these three areas of our lives.

And as we walk this life with all its up and downs, help us to remember who we are, where we are from, and where we are going.

In Jesus' name,

Amen.

Endnotes

Chapter 1

1. Stix, G., "The Neuroscience of True Grit", *Scientific American* 304, 2011, pp. 28–33: http://www.nature.com/scientificamerican/journal/v304/n3/full/scientificamerican0311-28.html

2. Newman, T., *Promoting Resilience: A Review of Effective Strategies for Child Care Services*, Exeter: Centre for Evidence-Based Social Services, University of Exeter, 2002.

3. Visinel's story was recounted by Wendell Steavenson who visited Romania in 1990. The article, entitled "Ceauşescu's children", appeared in *The Guardian* 10 December 2014: https://www.theguardian.com/news/2014/dec/10/-sp-ceausescus-children

4. McGinn, C., "Can We Solve the Mind-Body Problem?", *Mind*, 98, 1989, pp. 349–66.

5. Alexander, J. C., *The Meanings of Social Life: A Cultural Sociology*, Oxford: Oxford University Press, 2005.

6. Sheldrake, P., *A Brief History of Spirituality*, Oxford: Blackwell Publishing, 2007, p. 2.

7. Gray, R., "Grief leaves the body at risk of infection", *The Daily Telegraph*, 25 March 2002.

Chapter 2

1. Engel, G. L., "The Need for a New Medical Model: A Challenge for Biomedicine", *Science* 196, 1977, pp. 129–36.

2. Sometimes a person's mental health is as important as their physical health. What about a patient who has suicidal intent or severe depression?

3. Engel, G. L., "The Need for a New Medical Model: A Challenge for Biomedicine", *Science* 196, 1977, pp. 129–36.

4. WHO, The Ottawa Charter for Health Promotion, Geneva: WHO, 1986. http://www.who.int/healthpromotion/conferences/previous/ottawa/en/index.html.

5. The Ottawa Charter launched "Health for All" which was a series of health promotion goals for all people by the year 2000. It was to include international organizations, national governments, and local communities to deliver the plan.

6. Nightingale, F., *Notes on Nursing*, London: Hamson, 1882, p. 148.

7. Smuts J. C., *Holism and Evolution*, New York: Macmillan, 1926.

8. Patterson, E. F., "The philosophy and physics of holistic health care: Spiritual healing as a workable interpretation", *Journal of Advanced Nursing* 27, 1998, pp. 287–93.

9. Watson J., *Postmodern Nursing and Beyond*, Edinburgh: Churchill-Livingstone, 1999.

10. In Latin, "Cogito ergo sum". For more on Descartes' philosophy, see Lilli Alanen, *Descartes' Concept of Mind*, Cambridge: Harvard University Press, 2003.

11. "Entire" added by me.

12. Bohm, D., *Wholeness and the Implicate Order*, London & New York: Routledge & Kegan Paul, 1980, p. xvi.

Chapter 3

1. Epstein, R. M. & Krasner, M. S., "Physician resilience: what it means, why it matters, and how to promote it", *Academic Medicine* 2013, 88: pp. 301–303.

2. Davy, J., "Measuring Physical Resilience", 2011: http://www.investigage.com/2011/12/23/measuring-physical-resilience/

3. Charney, D. S. & Nemeroff, C. B., *The Peace of Mind Prescription: An Authoritative Guide to Finding the Most Effective Treatment for Anxiety and Depression*, Boston/New York: Houghton Mifflin Company, 2004.

4. NHS Choices, "Physical activity guidelines for adults", 2014: http://www.nhs.uk/Livewell/fitness/Pages/physical-activity-guidelines-for-adults.aspx

5. WHO, "Global Strategy on Diet, Physical Activity and Health", 2014: http://www.who.int/dietphysicalactivity/factsheet_adults/en/

6. Taylor, A. H. & Oliver, A., "Acute effects of brisk walking on urges to eat chocolate, affect, and responses to a stressor and chocolate cue. An experimental study", *Appetite* 2009, 52: 155–160.

7. Barton, J. & Pretty, J., "What is the best dose of nature and green exercise for improving mental health? A multi-study analysis", *Environmental Science & Technology* 2010, 44: 3947–55.

8. Guidry, M. A., Blanchard B. E., Thompson P. D., Maresh C. M., Seip R. L., Taylor A. L., & Pescatello L. S., "The influence of short and long duration on the blood pressure response to an acute bout of dynamic exercise", *American Heart Journal*, 2006, 151: 1322.e5–12.

9. Harvard Mental Health Letter, "Yoga for anxiety and depression", 2009: http://www.health.harvard.edu/mind-and-mood/yoga-for-anxiety-and-depression

10. See Hellerstein, D., "How Can I Become More Resilient?", 2011: http://www.psychologytoday.com/blog/heal-your-brain/201108/how-can-i-become-more-resilient

11. NHS Choices, "Eating a balanced diet", 2016: http://www.nhs.uk/livewell/goodfood/pages/healthyeating.aspx

12. Soell, G. , "Sport in Catholic Theology in the 20th Century", in O. Grupe, D. Kurz & J. M. Teipel (eds.), *The Scientific View of Sport*, New York: Springer Verlag, 1972, p. 63.

Chapter 4

1. http://www.merriam-webster.com/dictionary/rest

2. For more information about this read "Active Versus Passive Recovery": http://www.bodyrecomposition.com/training/active-versus-passive-recovery.html/

3. Popova, M., "The Theology of Rest: A Modern Sermon About Living with Presence in the Age of Productivity": https://www.brainpickings.org/2014/06/17/theology-of-rest/

4. http://www.oxforddictionaries.com/definition/english/sleep

5. For more information read Miller, M., Wright, H., Hough, J., & Cappuccio, F., "Sleep and Cognition" in Idzikowski, C. (ed.): *Sleep and its Disorders Affect Society*, InTech, 2014. A PDF of the "Sleep and Cognition" chapter (last accessed September 2016) is available at: http://www2.warwick.ac.uk/fac/med/research/mhwellbeing/sleep/sleeppublications/sleep_and_cognition_2014.pdf

6. Ross, J. J., "Neurological Findings After Prolonged Sleep Deprivation", *Archives of Neurology*, 1965, 12: 399–403.

7. Timms, P., "Sleeping Well", UK: The Royal College of Psychiatrists, 2014.

8. Gallagher, P., "Slavery in the City: Death of 21-year-old intern Moritz Erhardt at Merrill Lynch sparks furore over long hours and macho culture at banks", *The Independent*, August 2013: http://www.independent.co.uk/news/uk/home-news/slavery-in-the-city-death-of-21-year-old-intern-moritz-erhardt-at-merrill-lynch-sparks-furore-over-8775917.html

9. Chung, F., "The country working itself to death", March 2015: http://www.news.com.au/finance/work/at-work/the-country-working-itself-to-death/news-story/5c29cd052ce1b58e14247fc5f349163b

10. Harnois, G. & Phyllis, G., "Mental health and work: Impact, issues and good practices", WHO: Geneva, 2000: http://www.who.int/mental_health/media/en/712.pdf

11. Ruddick, G., "Chinese gamer dies after playing World of Warcraft for 19 hours", *The Telegraph*, March 2015: http://www.telegraph.co.uk/technology/11449055/Chinese-gamer-dies-after-playing-World-of-Warcraft-for-19-hours.html

12. For more information on this topic, see Josef Pieper, *Leisure: The Basis of Culture*, Munich: Kösel-Verlag, 1948. Originally translated into English by Alexander Dru, with an Introduction by T. S. Eliot, and published by Faber and Faber, London, 1952. A more recent translation is available by Gerald Malsbary, South Bend: St. Augustine's Press, 1998.

13. Pieper, J., *Leisure: The Basis of Culture*, Munich: Kösel-Verlag, 1948. Originally translated into English by Alexander Dru, with an Introduction by T. S. Eliot, and published by Faber and Faber, London, 1952.

14. Russell, B., *In Praise of Idleness: And Other Essays*, London: Routledge, 2004, p. 3.

15. Kreeft, P., "Confessions of a Computer Hater": http://www. peterkreeft.com/topics-more/computer-confessions.htm

16. Ferguson, S., "Sabbath Rest", Ligonier Ministries (The Teaching Fellowship of R. C. Sproul), 2016: http://www.ligonier.org/learn/ articles/sabbath-rest/

17. Brueggemann, W., *Sabbath as Resistance: Saying No to the Culture of Now*, Louisville, Kentucky: Westminster John Knox Press, 2014.

18. http://old.qideas.org/blog/wisdom-and-sabbath-rest.aspx

Chapter 5

1. WHO, "Mental Health: A Call for Action by the World Health Ministers", Geneva: WHO, 2001.

2. Mental Health Foundation, 2016; see https://www.mentalhealth.org. uk/your-mental-health/about-mental-health/what-mental-health

3. Cozolino, L., *The Neuroscience of Human Relationships*, New York: W. W. Norton & Company Ltd., 2006.

4. Walsh, F., *Strengthening Family Resilience*, New York: The Guildford Press, 2006.

5. Pargament, K. I., Mahoney, A. E., Shafranske, E. P., Exline, J. J., & Jones, J. W. (eds), *From research to practice: Toward an applied psychology of religion and spirituality*, Washington, DC: American Psychological Association, 2013.

6. Groeschel, C., *Soul Detox: Clean Living in a Contaminated World*, Grand Rapids: Zondervan, 2013.

Chapter 6

1. Lovecraft, H. P., *Supernatural Horror in Literature*, New York, NY: Dover, 1973: p. 12.

2. McFarland, D. (ed.), *The Oxford Companion to Animal Behaviour*, Oxford, UK: Oxford University Press, 1987.

3. Bush, D., Sotres-Bayon, F., & LeDoux, J., "Individual differences in fear: Isolating fear reactivity and fear recovery phenotypes", *Journal of Traumatic Stress* 2007; 20: pp. 413–22.

4. The University of Exeter, "Power of the subconscious in human fear revealed", *ScienceDaily*, 18 January 2012: www.sciencedaily.com/releases/2012/01/120118101538.htm

5. Steimer, T., "The biology of fear- and anxiety-related behaviors", *Dialogues in Clinical Neuroscience*, 2002, 4: pp. 231–49: http://www.ncbi.nlm.nih.gov/pmc/articles/PMC3181681/pdf/DialoguesClinNeurosci-4-231.pdf

6. Craig, K. J., Brown, K.J., & Baum, A., "Environmental factors in the etiology of anxiety", in Bloom, F. E. & Kupfer, D. J. (eds), *Psychopharmacology: The Fourth Generation of Progress,* New York, NY: Raven Press, 1995: 1325–39.

7. Barlow, D. H., "Unraveling the mysteries of anxiety and its disorders from the perspective of emotion theory", *The American Psychologist* 2000; 55:1247–63.

8. Craig K. J., Brown K. J., & Baum A., "Environmental factors in the etiology of anxiety" in Bloom F. E., & Kupfer D. J., (eds), *Psychopharmacology: the Fourth Generation of Progress.* New York, NY: Raven Press; 1995: 1325–39.

9. *Ibid.*

10. See https://www.theibsnetwork.org/.

11. Roest, A., Martens, E., de Jonge, P., & Denollet, J., "Anxiety and risk of incident coronary heart disease: a meta-analysis", *Journal of the American College of Cardiology 2010*; 56:38–46 and Janszky, I., Ahnve, S., Lundberg, I., & Hemmingsson, T., "Early-onset depression, anxiety and risk of subsequent coronary heart disease: 37-year follow-up of 49,321 young Swedish men", *Journal of the American College of Cardiology* 2010; 56:31–37.

12. Habakkuk 3:18.

13. Psalm 91:2.

14. Psalm 39:7.

Chapter 7

1. Mind, "How many people have mental health problems?", 2016: http://www.mind.org.uk/information-support/types-of-mental-health-problems/statistics-and-facts-about-mental-health/how-common-are-mental-health-problems/

2. Mind, "Improving mental health training for GPs and practice nurses. Better equipped, better care.", 2016, p. 6: http://www.mind.org.uk/media/5063246/find-the-words-report-better-equipped-better-care.pdf

3. http://www.transmhs.org/the-facts-about-mental-health.php

4. Mind, "How many people have mental health problems?", 2016, http://www.mind.org.uk/information-support/types-of-mental-health-problems/statistics-and-facts-about-mental-health/how-common-are-mental-health-problems/

5. Sedghi, A., "What is the state of children's mental health today?", *The Guardian*: www.theguardian.com/society/christmas-charity-appeal-2014-blog/2015/jan/05/-sp-state-children-young-people-mental-health-today

6. Merriam–Webster, Medical Dictionary, http://www.merriam-Webster.com/medical/mental%20illness

7. Wakefield, J. C., "The concept of mental disorder: On the boundary between biological facts and social values", *American Psychologist* 1992; 47:(3) 373–88. http://isites.harvard.edu/fs/docs/icb.topic625827.files/Wakefield%20-%20harmful%20dysfunction.pdf

8. Chisholm, D. & Saxena, S., "Depression, A global public health concern", 2012: http://www.who.int/mental_health/management/depression/who_paper_depression_wfmh_2012.pdf

9. Favazza, A. R., "Modern Christian healing of mental illness", *American Journal of Psychiatry* 1982; 139: 728–35.

10. Warner, R., *Recovery from Schizophrenia: Psychiatry and Political Economy*, Routledge: London, 2004, p. 173.

11. Goffman, E., *Stigma: Notes on the Management of Spoiled Identity*, Prentice-Hall: Englewood Cliffs, NJ, 1963.

12. Link, B. G., Struening, E. L., Rahav, M., Phelan, J. C., & Nuttbrock, L., "On stigma and its consequences: evidence from a longitudinal study of men with dual diagnoses of mental illness and substance abuse", *Journal of Health and Social Behavior* 1997; 38: 177–90.

13. Link, B. G. & Phelan, J. C., "Conceptualizing stigma", *Annual Review of Sociology* 2001; 27: 363–85.

14. Feldman, D. B. & Crandall, C. S., "Dimensions of mental illness stigma: what about mental illness causes social rejection?", *Journal of Social and Clinical Psychology*, 2007; 26: 137–54.

15. Aromaa, E., Tolvanen, A., Tuulari, J., & Wahlbeck, K., "Personal stigma and use of mental health services among people with depression in a general population in Finland", *BMC Psychiatry* 2011; 11: 52–57.

16. For further information read LifeWay's 2014 research report, "Study of Acute Mental Illness and Christian Faith": http://lifewayresearch.com/wp-content/uploads/2014/09/Acute-Mental-Illness-and-Christian-Faith-Research-Report-1.pdf. See also Bob Smietana, "Mental health remains taboo topic for many pastors", LifeWay Research, 2014: http://lifewayresearch.com/2014/09/22/mental-illness-remains-taboo-topic-for-many-pastors/

17. Jongbloed, A., "4 Misconceptions About Mental Illness and Faith", *Relevant* magazine, December 2014: http://www.relevantmagazine.com/god/church/4-misconceptions-about-mental-illness-and-faith

18. Simpson, A., *Troubled Minds: Mental Illness and the Church's Mission*, InterVarsity Press: Downers Grove, IL, 2013.

19. Stanford, M. S., "Demon or disorder: A survey of attitudes toward mental illness in the Christian church", *Mental Health, Religion and Culture*, 2007; 10: 445–49.

20. Stetzer, E., "A New Approach to Mental Illness in the Church", *Christianity Today*, 10 April 2015: http://www.christianitytoday.com/edstetzer/2015/april/new-approach-to-mental-illness-in-church.html

21. Mind and Soul: http://www.mindandsoul.info/Groups/108634/Mind_and_Soul.aspx

22. Quoted by Lodge, C., "How can we tackle the stigma around mental

health?", *Christian Today*, 14 August 2014: http://www.christiantoday.
com/article/how.can.we.tackle.stigma.around.mental.health/39597.
htm

23. Stanford, M. S., "Demon or disorder: A survey of attitudes toward
mental illness in the Christian church", *Mental Health, Religion and
Culture* 2007; 10: 445–49.

Chapter 8

1. Yeung, D. & Martin, M., *Spiritual Fitness and Resilience: A Review of
Relevant Constructs, Measures, and Links to Well-Being*, RAND Project
AIR FORCE Series on Resiliency, RAND Corporation: USA, 2013.
Full report available at: http://www.rand.org/content/dam/rand/pubs/
research_reports/RR100/RR100/RAND_RR100.pdf

2. Hackney, C. & Sanders, G., "Religiosity and Mental Health: A Meta-
Analysis of Recent Studies", *Journal for the Scientific Study of Religion*
2003; 42: 43–55.

3. Young & Martin, *Spiritual Fitness and Resilience*, RAND Project AIR
FORCE Series on Resiliency, RAND Corporation: USA, 2013.

4. Hart, J., "Clinical applications for meditation: a review and
recommendations", *Alternative and Complementary Therapies* 2007;
14:24–29.

5. Moberg, D., "Research in spirituality, religion, and aging", *Journal of
Gerontological Social Work* 2005; 45: 11–40.

6. Tshabalala, B. G. & Patel, C. J., "The role of praise and worship
activities in spiritual well-being: Perceptions of a Pentecostal Youth
Ministry group", *International Journal of Children's Spirituality*, 2010;
15: 73–82.

7. Foster, R., *Celebration of Discipline: The Path to Spiritual Growth*,
London: Hodder & Stoughton, 2008.

8. For more information go to https://renovare.org/about/overview

9. Zanzig, T., *Christian Meditation for Beginners* (ed. M. Kielbasa),
Winona, Minnesota: Saint Mary's Press, 2000: p. 7.

10. St Teresa of Avila, *Interior Castle*, edited and translated by E. Allison

Peers, Mineola, NY: Dover Publications Inc., 1946, p. 124.

11. McGrath, A., *Christian Spirituality: An Introduction*, Oxford: Wiley-Blackwell, 2011, p. 88.

12. Cohn, M., Fredrickson, B., Brown, S., Mikels, J., & Conway, A., "Happiness Unpacked: Positive Emotions Increase Life Satisfaction by Building Resilience", *Emotion* 2009; 9: 361–68.

13. Read more about The Complaint Free World Project here: http://www.willbowen.com/

14. Lally, P., van Jaarsfeld, C., Potts, H., & Wardle, J., "How are habits formed: Modelling habit formation in the real world", *European Journal of Social Psychology* 2009; 40: 998–1009.

15. The Evangelical Alliance, *21st Century Evangelicals: Time for discipleship?*, 2014: http://www.eauk.org/church/resources/snapshot/loader.cfm?csModule=security/getfile&PageID=49835

16. Hansen, R. & Wall, D., "Why People Don't Pray", *Leadership Journal*, Autumn 1994: http://www.christianitytoday.com/le/1994/fall/4l4061.html

Chapter 9

1. NHS, "NHS Health Check": http://www.nhs.uk/Conditions/nhs-health-check/Pages/NHS-Health-Check.aspx

2. http://www.cslewisinstitute.org/2016_Annual_Spiritual_Checkup

3. Partridge, T., CWR "Spiritual Health Check", 2016: http://www.cwr.org.uk/doc/pdfs/SpiritualHealthCheck.pdf

Chapter 10

1. For more about Scripture Union, see http://www.scriptureunion.org.uk/8.id

2. Joni Eareckson Tada, *Joni: An Unforgettable Story*, Grand Rapids, MI: Zondervan, 1976.

3. For more information see the website: https://freechurch.org/

Chapter 11

1. Rainolds, J., *Zeal a Virtue: Or, A Discourse Concerning Sacred Zeal*, London: John Clark, 1716, p. 18.

2. Brown, B., *The Power of Vulnerability*, Audiobook, Sounds True Inc., 2013.

3. Ibid.

4. See http://www.aifc.com.au/blockages-to-healing-and-growth-unforgiveness-2/

5. Fenner, W., *A Treatise of the Affections*, London, 1650, p. 162.

6. Marano, H. E., "The art of resilience", Psychology Today, 2003: https://www.psychologytoday.com/articles/200305/the-art-resilience. Accessed 21 September 2016.

Chapter 12

1. Watch it at https://www.youtube.com/watch?v=8YcvuxN-T28

2. Definition according to the Oxford English Dictionary: https://en.oxforddictionaries.com/definition/perseverance

3. Fordyce, T., "How the world's elite sprinters prepare for a race", BBC sport, 2010. http://www.bbc.co.uk/blogs/tomfordyce/2010/05/inside_the_mind_of_a_topclass.html

4. See http://www.desertrunnersmovie.com/film/

Chapter 13

1. Brown, B., *Rising Strong*, London: Ebury, 2015.